The Revd Dr Sharon Prentis is the Intercultural Mission Enabler and Dean of Black, Asian and Minority Ethnic Affairs in the Church of England, Birmingham, and Honorary Research Fellow at the Edward Cadbury Centre for the Public Understanding of Religion, University of Birmingham. Sharon has worked as an associate priest in Essex and as a lecturer at St Mellitus College, London, and at the Universities of Leeds and Huddersfield, where she was involved in community-based projects. Her research was recognized by the Department of Health when she was named as a Mary Seacole Scholar for her contribution to faith and health. She continues to work with others to promote diversity and inclusion in the Church of England.

To those of you called
to be saints

Sharon Prentis

October 2019.

D1646300

edited by Sharon Prentis

every tribe

stories of diverse
saints serving a
diverse world

First published in Great Britain in 2019

Society for Promoting Christian Knowledge
36 Causton Street
London SW1P 4ST
www.spck.org.uk

British Library Cataloguing-in-Publication Data
A catalogue record for this book is available from the British Library

ISBN 978–0–281–08085–4
eBook ISBN 978–0–281–08084–7

Typeset by Manila Typesetting Company
First printed in Great Britain by Jellyfish Print Solutions
Subsequently digitally reprinted in Great Britain

eBook by Manila Typesetting Company

Produced on paper from sustainable forests

Contents

Contents

*To Loreen and all the 'ordinary' saints throughout history
whose stories are never told.*

*They are the 'righteous ones' (Hebrew: tzadikim)
whose faithfulness is in acts of everyday holiness known
only to God.*

*Unseen, they persevere in the name of Christ,
faithful disciples contending with major challenges, often at
great cost.*

*They belong to the great communion of saints made up of
every tribe, nation and tongue,
who together reflect the glory of God and are just as holy as
their better-known counterparts*

In a time of increasing extremism of all kinds it is good to be reminded that Christ's sacrifice enables the inclusion of everyone.

Preface

Sharon Prentis

The idea for a book on saints and holy people emerged from a lively discussion at the Church of England's Committee for Minority Ethnic Anglican Concerns (CMEAC). For nearly three decades it has worked to encourage the full participation of diverse people in the life of the Church. Various initiatives over that time have resulted in modest success, but there is still some way to go before a truly representative Church is a reality. To mark the committee's thirtieth year, one suggestion was to highlight the lives of holy people throughout the ages who had originated outside Europe and whose stories of faith might interest others. We were aware that our Christian heritage included diverse men and women of inspiring faith whose stories were not often heard. These holy ones, motivated by their faith, lived contrary to the prevailing norms, expectations and customs of the times, in some circumstances at the cost of their lives. What they had in common was the separation of their stories not only from their countries of origin but also from their cultural identity. History had relocated them, ignoring or reframing their narratives in ways that took little account of their ethnic heritage or social status. As a result, the impact of their unique contributions to the faith tradition is diminished.

Their wisdom has its foundation in the dynamic life of the Trinity – the community we are invited to join and be in fellowship with. No one can be saintly by him- or herself. Belonging to a diverse array of witnesses challenges our tendency towards self-defined piety – what it should look like and, more importantly, that it should instead rely on dependence on God and interdependence on each other. Christians should never be what Dietrich Bonhoeffer terms a 'community of the pious', exclusive in attitude and inward-orientated. Instead, the Christian community seeks to be like Christ in the midst of a broken world and culture that sees the gospel as trivial at best and offensive at worst. Furthermore, being together in Christian community acknowledges that we are a work in progress, daily pursuing holiness rather than maintain the façade of striving to perfection.

'Christian community is like the Christian's sanctification. It is a gift of God which we cannot claim. Only God knows the real state of our fellowship, of our sanctification.'[1]

This is further emphasized when remembering that the word 'community' shares the same root as 'communion': the coming together with one another and ultimately with God.

Among the many examples of inspired souls, the ones identified here have made a particular impression. Some historical individuals like George, patron saint of England, are familiar; others, like St Hadrian, the sixth-century abbot of Canterbury, and St Alphonsa, nun and educator from India, are unknown. Such was the interest in their stories that an aim to introduce them to a wider audience emerged. However, the intention was not just to relate their biographies in the usual fashion, but to retell them from the perspectives of narrators who identified with their values and who, like them, had origins or connections in other parts of the world. In a time of increasing extremism of all kinds, it is good to be reminded that Christ's sacrifice enables the inclusion of everyone.

By selecting some saints, it is inevitable that others are left out. Those chosen represent the eternal kingdom values of righteousness, love, humility, selfless service, hope, redemption and restoration. Each biography is accompanied by a reflection or prayer to help the reader consider what it is to be holy. Questions found at the end of the book are intended to help provoke further thinking about what it means to live in contemporary society where there are numerous challenges to holiness in everyday life.

In acknowledging their contributions to the faith, the intention of this book is not to elevate certain individuals and set them apart from us, nor is it to suggest that they are unusually gifted by God. Instead, it is to recognize their diverse humanity;

people of grace who stood firm in their faith. They too, like us, were following a call to holy living, pursuing it with integrity and through difficult times. As we get to know their stories, inevitably we see God and appreciate that we too can be a part of the holy band of saints. We are all called. No extraordinary human abilities are required; rather, it is the willingness to obey the call from a holy God to be a holy people.

Acknowledgements

My thanks go to the Committee for Minority Ethnic Anglican Concerns (CMEAC), particularly Elizabeth Henry, for their encouragement and unwavering commitment to see the whole people of God find their place in the Church.

Special thanks to Sheila Varghese for her willingness to read, format and contribute to the content. Sheila, without your generosity this project would remain just an interesting idea. Thank you for enabling the call to inform and encourage.

Finally, we give thanks for all the saints who have gone before, and those still living, whose stories continue to inspire us daily by directing our gaze to God.

every
tribe

Their inspired lives
can inspire us today
and help the Church
to become what it
is meant to be: the
rainbow people of God
serving the diverse
needs of a diverse
world.

Introduction by the Bishop of Chelmsford

What exactly is a saint?

Christian people approach the term with a certain trepidation. On the one hand, we are all saints. It is the word Paul often uses to describe those who through faith in Christ are members of his Church.

It means holy. That's not necessarily a special holiness that only certain people achieve. The holiness Paul is referring to is that which comes in 'with one great gulp of grace' (to use St Cyprian's words) when we receive the spirit of Christ.

But on the other hand, and from the earliest times, the Church has found it fitting to honour and remember the particular lives of particular Christians whose general holiness was so focused and alert that Christ himself seemed to be revealed in them in ways that had eluded the rest of us.

From the first martyr, Stephen, to those whose lives are violently wrenched from them in our own age of persecution, Christians who have witnessed to their faith even to death have been remembered. So, too, church leaders and pioneers, teachers and evangelists: their names fill our calendars, and the stories of their lives continue to inspire and direct. In the manifold details of ten thousand times ten thousand particular lives, they show us what a Christian life looks like.

In this respect, the trepidation falls away. All are saints; and all are called to be saints, in so far as to be a saint is not to be especially chosen or equipped over and above any other Christian disciple, but simply and supremely to have fully become the person one is called to be. W. H. Auden observed in his wonderful poem, 'In Praise of Limestone', that saints don't need to care what angle they are viewed from, because they have nothing to hide.[1]

Nevertheless, the usually effete and idealized images of saints in our stained-glass windows and their stories in overly sentimental hagiographies mean that many Christians do consider saints to be separate from the rest of us. The lingering influence of a certain sort of medieval theology that saw them as useful mediators between humanity and Christ has not helped.

In the Creed we declare a belief in the communion of saints. First and foremost, this simply means we believe that heaven belongs to all of us because of what God has done in Christ. It is our homeland. The saints are those who dwell with God. They show us our destiny.

Therefore, I do not have any problem in asking for their prayers. I am not asking them to mediate on my behalf because I cannot go directly to Christ myself. Asking for the prayer of the saints should be as normal as asking for the prayer of my friends in Christ. The saints *are my friends in Christ*: the Church in heaven, in all its colourful diversity, unites its voice with the Church on earth.

But this biblical vision has another vital but often neglected dimension. Something this little book aims to put right. In the book of Revelation it says that in the new heaven and the new earth there will be people – saints is the actual word used – of every tribe and language and people and nation (see Revelation 5.9 and 7.9). It is a vision of glorious diversity and inclusion.

In which case, why are all the saints in our stained-glass windows white? And why are even the black ones, like Augustine or Athanasius, depicted as if they were white? A scandalously oppressive bias has been allowed to take hold of the iconography and storytelling of the Church, and this has even bleached our corporate memory, so that now – as you may be when reading this book – people are surprised, even shocked, to discover that St Augustine was from present-day Algeria, that the great doctors of the Church, Athanasius and Cyril, were Egyptian, that Cyprian, whom I quoted above, was Tunisian, and that even that most British of saints, George, was an immigrant with a Turkish father and a Palestinian mother. And this is even before we have told the story of twentieth- and twenty-first-century saints and martyrs like Janani Luwum from Uganda or Esther John from Pakistan.

We may be surrounded by a great cloud of witnesses, but the black and Asian faces in the crowd have been hidden in the fog of white, male, Anglo-Saxon bias. And the faces that can be seen have all been spiritually enhanced to conform to a white, European theological hegemony.

This must change. It must change because it is wrong. It must change because it is unjust. It must change because it fatally damages the credibility and witness of the Church, contributing to a still prejudiced culture in the Church today, evidenced by the lack of black and global majority faces in the leadership of the Church.

But these glorious black saints did live and breathe and witness to Christ, and became channels through which Christ's ministry was continued. In so doing they became the people they were meant to be, and did not mind what angle they were regarded from. Warts and all, and very mindful of the need of God, their inspired lives can inspire us today and help the Church to become what it is meant to be: the rainbow people of God serving the diverse needs of a diverse world.

Stephen Cottrell, Bishop of Chelmsford

In a context where religious intolerance is growing, St George challenges the world to be tolerant and hospitable.

St George, Patron Saint of England

(270–303)

John Perumbalath

The Rt Revd Dr John Perumbalath is the Bishop of Bradwell in Essex. A British Asian, he comes from the ancient Syrian Christian community in Kerala, South India. Ordained in the Church of North India in 1994, he was a theological educator and parish priest based in Kolkata until his move to the UK in 2001. After serving as a parish priest in the diocese of Rochester, he moved to East London in 2013 as Archdeacon of Barking. He has served on the General Synod of the Church of England and chaired the Committee for Minority Ethnic Anglican Concerns (CMEAC). He lectures widely in the areas of biblical interpretation, urban pastoral practice and Christian social engagement.

St George and English nationality are often inextricably linked. In reality, St George was a Palestinian Christian, who according to Greek tradition was born to Christian parents in Cappadocia, Turkey around AD 270. While George was still a child, he and his mother fled to Palestine after George's father died for his faith, a persecution George would later experience for himself.

So how did George, a young man growing up in Palestine and later serving in the Roman army, become the patron saint of England? From the little we know of him, we understand that his faith was dynamic, one of compassion, defending the poor and the helpless. He was a warrior, but one of peace. Arguably the most famous story about him – one of the many stories told by the medieval Eastern Orthodox Church, brought back to Europe by the Crusaders in the tenth and eleventh centuries – concerns his slaying of a dragon.

One version tells of a plague-infected dragon living in a lake near a town in Libya. Day after day the townspeople were being killed by the dragon. St George happened to ride past the town and, on hearing the misery of the townspeople, offered to slay the dragon in one heroic act of compassion, the whole town giving their lives to Christ as a result. In many ways, this story can be seen as an allegory of God's care for human suffering and the deliverance of the Church from persecution, with the dragon a symbol of evil, possibly deriving from the book of Revelation (12.9). The story is about compassion for people, defence of the poor and the intervening mercy of God.

King Richard I called upon St George, renowned for his bravery, for protection before the Third Crusade in 1187. Around this time a red cross on a white background became the 'uniform' for the Crusaders, a symbol that even today remains closely linked with the person of St George. It wasn't, however, until King Edward III came to the throne in 1327 that St George was made the official saint of England at the establishment of the Order of the Garter. For Edward III, this was part of rebranding and rebuilding England after the disastrous reign of his father. St George was seen to symbolize the strength of the English monarchy, his exploits affirming England as a powerful nation. Since Edward III, a religious cult of St George was promoted and the secular cult of St George the hero was created in order to foster loyalty to the Crown and develop a sense of national identity. Several myths and traditions surrounding St George have grown over the last 17 centuries, meaning it is hard to ensure their factual accuracy. What is astoundingly clear, however, is that George was a man with a complex heritage, born as cultures and empires were colliding. In addition to England, he became the patron saint of Catalonia, Greece, Lithuania, Russia, Bulgaria, Ethiopia, Georgia and many others, as the St George tradition took various shapes and was promoted by the Crusaders.

George also became a saint in Palestine in a short span of time and was venerated together with Moses, Elijah and Michael for his exemplary bravery, as a defender of women and the poor, and an upholder of the Christian faith, something George did until his very last breath. Following his mother's death, George used his inheritance to establish himself at the court of the Emperor Diocletian in Constantinople. In 303, the Emperor Diocletian issued an edict that all Christian soldiers in the army should be expelled and all soldiers make the traditional pagan sacrifice. Indicative of the man he was to become, a bold young George refused in front of his fellow soldiers and confessed his faith publicly, even rejecting the Emperor's attempts to convert George with offers of wealth. Refusing to deny his beliefs, George was tortured, and finally decapitated on 23 April 303 in the town of Lydda (now Lod in Israel). He became known throughout the East as 'The Great Martyr'. Despite his unapologetic affirmation of the Christian faith, St George is revered by Christians and Muslims alike across the Middle East, many of whom visit an Eastern Orthodox shrine of St George at Beith Jala, near Jerusalem. Jews visit too believing that Elijah was buried there. We can be sure, therefore, that nothing that we know of St George lends itself to narrow patriotism, hatred and communal conflict.

Despite George's adoption by many diverse cultures, a patron saint does not have to be from the country in which they were born. They do, however, need to embody the characteristics the country wants to embrace and shape its image around.

Whatever the intentions of King Edward III in adopting St George as the patron saint of England, one finds today that George is a perfect fit for England as a multiracial man of the world who can speak the dozens of languages one would hear on the streets of England every day.

Though his multicultural identity may be embraced by the diverse people who walk England's streets, his outspokenness might not. Today, our society expects individuals, especially public figures, to keep their religion a private matter. St George was instead unashamedly Christian and in a very public way. He was a witness to Christ and keen to draw people to God.

Faith in the public square is becoming a real challenge for Christians and the Church today. St George's example represents effective and fruitful engagement of the Christian faith with public spaces. In a world where Christians were a tiny minority, and in a variety of geographical and cultural situations, St George engaged with communities and authorities. That his faith led to his martyrdom is a reminder of the cost of discipleship in the public square.

St George, so often domesticated for narrow nationalistic gains, should instead be seen as a brave man, bold in speaking about the faith and international in his appeal and acceptance, with communities in England sharing this Palestinian Roman saint with many other communities and nationalities around the world.

Personal reflections

Immigration is the talk of the hour in Great Britain today. Political discourses around us are encouraging a tendency to blame 'the immigrants' for everything. What would St George say to England today? George had to move from Cappadocia to Palestine following his father's death, probably to be employed as a palace guard for the Emperor Diocletian. He moved between the provinces of the vast Roman Empire and he could surely understand how skilled manual workers travel between the member states of the EU to find better employment. And this patron saint is a migrant to England from Palestine, although not literally – he never came to England – but in the way society in England has adopted him and built English traditions around him.

This Palestinian saint, both mythical and multicultural, can and should be an icon of the new Englishness that embraces cultural and religious diversity. St George today should serve as a warning against narrow nationalism and blinkered patriotism. In a context where religious intolerance is growing, St George challenges the world to be tolerant and hospitable. St George can be not only an inspiration for England but also a challenge to contemporary society to redefine its identity and vision.

Prayer

Lord God, you who called George with his diverse background
    to be a force of good for you,
and to turn the hearts of people towards you.
You who are much bigger than we can think or imagine,
give us the humility needed to accept our communities;
grant us the willingness to engage in dialogue with those different from us.
Help us take our communities seriously because they matter
    to you.

May we be able to capture the imagination of people everywhere
with your timeless story.
To place your story alongside their own,
and help them realize that your story is powerful and challenging;
it continually offers them and us hope and assurance.
Help us go to out as did your servant, George,
with humility and courage, to not only tell them your story
but to show it to them by our lives and actions.
Amen.

He lived and taught
that the ultimate goal
of the life of prayer is to
achieve purity of heart.

Abba Moses

(330–405)

Calvert Prentis

Calvert Prentis was born in Yorkshire of African-Caribbean parents. After several years working as an upholsterer, Calvert was ordained in the Church of England.

Since 1997, he has been involved in mentoring and served as a priest in parish ministry in urban, suburban and city-centre contexts. He now works as Diocesan Director of Ordinands and Vocation Development in the Church of England, Birmingham, supporting individuals in discerning and developing their sense of call to ordained and authorized ministry. His desire is to see diverse congregations flourish and realize their vocation as Christ's followers.

The desert is a strange and unfamiliar place. With extremes of heat and scarce natural resources, it represented a number of physical and spiritual challenges for the early Christian men and women who chose to dwell there. In its stark conditions, they sought spiritual closeness with God. The Desert Fathers, as the men came to be known, were people who lived lives of great piety and simplicity despite the harsh realities of desert life. Much writing is devoted to them and the lessons they can teach us. But perhaps it is the contrast between their former lives and the change brought about by faith that captures the imagination and instils hope the most.

One story concerns St Moses the Ethiopian of Scete, who started out as a hardened criminal but went on to experience a remarkable Christian conversion. Also known as Moses the Black, or Abba Moses, he was born in the year 330 as a slave in the house of an important Egyptian official. After being thrown out of his master's household for dishonesty, Moses joined a gang of notorious thieves who were known for intimidating others. Due to his great strength, large stature, menacing presence and violent temperament, Moses soon became leader of the reputation gang and the mastermind behind several raids into the local countryside to ransack, steal from and murder the locals.

Such was his reputation for violence that he was feared by all. While on the run after a raid Moses took refuge in the monastery at Petra. His intention was to hide out there until he could rejoin his men on their rampages. However, at Petra he encountered a group of hermits who made such a deep impression on him that he vowed to give up his former villainous life to join them. His reputation, though, preceded him and the hermits were not convinced that such a hardened criminal could renounce a life of crime to pursue one of holiness. Despite their obvious reluctance to accept him, Moses persisted with his request to join the hermits. Eventually, after testing him to see if he would revert to his former ways, they became convinced of his change of heart and fervent desire to follow Christ. He too became a hermit, spending long periods alone in prayer, living in austerity and devoting himself to serving the older monks in the community.

However, the reality of his former life was not far away. One evening after his conversion, robbers tried to attack Moses at the monastery. The story goes that he fought four of them at once, overpowered them, tied them up and brought them before the head of his order. Asking the hermits what he should do with his attackers, his abbot replied, 'You should forgive them and let them go.' Moses agreed. The freed men were so astounded by the change in their former leader that they renounced their former lives to become monks. They found the contrast between his violent temperament and his new-found piety striking. By all accounts, Moses was a most unlikely person to be called a saint, and yet this man and his tendency towards violence became irrevocably changed by encountering people of faith and their God.

As a young man he recalled another monk, Antony the Great, considering the question of what characteristic or attribute could keep a monk protected from the snares and deceptions of the devil and enable him to attain holiness. As a result Abba Moses spent many years in solitary prayer trying to emulate the life of Christ and recognizing that without the Holy Spirit's help he could not be transformed. In experiencing the practical realities of the desert, he lived and taught that the ultimate goal of the life of prayer is to achieve purity of heart.

Even in old age Moses was an imposing yet gentle figure, gaining respect and love from others instead of the fear and intimidation of his earlier years. Abba Moses went on to mentor many brothers who lived on the fringes of society, and who saw by his example that they too could change. He was murdered in 405 by Berbers at Petra, Scete, Egypt. The power of transformation is not so much about the change in personality, but the ongoing influence the individual has on others. Among his many pieces of sage advice was this one concerning how to remain committed to the life of holiness:

> We give up country, family, possessions and everything worldly in order to acquire purity of heart. If we forget this purpose we cannot avoid frequently stumbling and losing our way, for we will be walking in the dark and straying from the proper path. This has happened to many men who at the start of their ascetic life gave up all wealth, possessions and everything worldly, but who later flew into a rage over a fork, a needle, a rush or a book. This would not have happened to them had they borne in mind the purpose for which they gave up everything.[1]

Personal reflections

I was born in Chapeltown, Leeds, a tough inner-city neighbour-hood that experienced riots, social unrest and had a reputation for crime. Some of my contemporaries went to prison – not all, but a few – but at the time that I was growing up most young black men were seen in a negative light. In a similar way to Moses, several individuals had made poor choices in their youth, but had seen the error of their ways and resolved to live their lives reflecting the glory of God. My peers who changed also sought to convince younger men that they were of worth and had something to contribute to the world.

Moses' transformation was not an easy one: he had to per-suade his new community and his old one that he had changed. Moses also fought his inclination to use intimidation, violence and manipulation. He saw this as a battle between good and evil, his own nature and his desires versus those longed-for characteristics of God: holiness, faithfulness and righteousness.

What strikes me the most about his life is the evidence of humility. On several occasions he confessed his unworthiness to receive God's grace. The memory of his former life was so predominant that, filled with remorse, he struggled to accept forgiveness. What is heartening is that he finally did, going on to influence the lives of others for good.

At a time when we are focusing on social and cultural iden-tities, voices of affirmation are mirrors that can reflect what we can be. To me, Abba Moses was such a man: someone who knew what it was to be negatively defined by others and whose acceptance by Christ and his disciples was able to challenge that expectation. Even though he was on the run, meeting the hermits must have been a complete contrast to what he had known; their lives and their message made a lasting impact on him. His humility was not false, but was born out of gratitude for Christ's ultimate sacrifice. Being born of no status, resorting to crime and choosing a lifestyle that involved intimidation and violence inevitably meant always having to assert his authority in the same way. After his conversion he was said to acknowledge that because of his past he expected his life to end violently, as it was no less than he deserved. He died at the hands of raiders after refusing to leave his monastery when warned of an imminent attack. His was a life marked by humility and grace for those who never let him forget his past; as such, he will never be forgotten.

Litany inspired by the humility of Abba Moses

Abba Father,

You call us out of darkness into your marvellous light to be like Christ and to share in your heavenly kingdom. Forgive us when we turn away from you towards our own desires.

By the power of your Holy Spirit, turn us:
From the limitation of our experiences, towards your eternal mercy.
Forgive us and restore us.

From our egos and selfish inclinations, towards your justice and righteousness.
Forgive us and restore us.

From our own sense of entitlement, towards your heart for the poor, disenfranchised and marginalized.

Forgive us and restore us.

From our selfishness to love those most like us, towards everyone your love fully embraces.

Forgive us and restore us.

From our tendency to strive to seek for approval for its own sake, towards dependence on your grace.

Forgive us and restore us.

From our propensity towards the violence and separation of hate, towards your reconciling peace.

Forgive us and restore us.

Create in us a clean heart and renew a right Spirit within us. Restore us in Jesus Christ our Lord. Amen.

Faith is to believe what we do not see; and the reward of this faith is to see what we believe.

St Augustine of Hippo

(354–430)

Sharon Prentis

History can sometimes fail to capture fully the magnitude and influence of an individual. One such figure in the great landscape of church history is St Augustine of Hippo. Philosopher, teacher, monk and bishop, he is celebrated as one of the early Fathers of the Christian Church, whose thoughts on original sin, the doctrine of grace and the Holy Spirit are still debated. However, it is the personal reflections of an African man's life captured in his *Confessions* – one of the earliest autobiographies – that continue to be a source of inspiration. During his lifetime his influence was confined to a relatively small area, but centuries later his written work has become an invaluable insight into medieval North African thought.

Augustine was born in Thagaste (Souk-Ahras), a Roman city in modern-day Algeria. Like the rest of the Roman Empire at the time, its subjects were made up of a variety of conquered peoples with the provinces reflecting a cosmopolitan and socially structured population. Although his family were Berbers (people who originated from a nomadic tribe), they were full Roman citizens;

and while not wealthy by any means, his father Patricius Aurelias was a respected town councillor, who spent most of his modest income on civic obligations through supporting public services. Although both parents were highly ambitious for their intellectually gifted son, it was Patricius who encouraged a high degree of self-indulgent behaviour in the young Augustine, seeing it as the natural self-expression of a curious mind and consistent with his own pagan values. In contrast, his mother Monica was a devout Christian, a woman of moral virtue who showed much patience in the face of her husband's pagan sympathies and open lifestyle. The couple, although having differing religious views, jointly encouraged their gifted son to acquire a classical education in Latin and Greek so that he could take full advantage of the opportunities the Roman Empire offered.

In his *Confessions*, Augustine admitted that as a young man he had no interest in his mother's faith, finding her beliefs unappealing. As an intellectual he was more interested in investigating the philosophical concepts then prevalent than Christianity. Yet, despite his keenness for ideas, he found his school lessons uninspiring. This reluctance to study often led him to get into trouble with tutors and be beaten with a rod, something he later vehemently complained about in his writings. Nevertheless, as a gifted student he developed a love for literature, especially the use of language, which became evident in the way he wrote, debated and preached. When he had finished his preliminary education at the age of 17 he was sent away to Carthage to pursue further studies. It was during that time that he enthusiastically explored other views and perspectives, and continued his self-indulgent pursuits.

After completing his studies, Augustine travelled to Rome and Milan to teach the rhetoric and philosophy that had so captivated him. He became a well-known orator, holding several key academic positions. However, despite becoming renowned as an intellectual and teacher, he could not escape the gnawing restlessness that had persisted for most of his life, and so he continued to investigate other ideas in his quest for answers.

The works of Cicero, Plato and abstract notions about human perfection and happiness led him to became a Manichean: a devout follower of an ancient religious cult. Manicheans believed that human will and actions were shaped by a struggle between good and evil. God was merely a bystander in the cosmic battle. However, Augustine soon became disenchanted with Manicheism and what he saw as the lack of intellectual rigour of its founder. All the while, Monica his mother continued to encourage him to explore the Christian faith. Although it was becoming more intellectually appealing to him, he concluded it was impossible to become a Christian.

Eventually, the cult lost its appeal and Augustine became disillusioned when its leader was unable to answer his questions. Augustine was once again in search of what seemed so elusive – a wisdom that made sense of his experience and intellectual questions. It was then he began to reconsider the faith of his mother and to explore Christianity seriously. With the encouragement of Monica and following prolonged conversations with the Bishop of Milan, St Ambrose, his conversion came soon after he experienced a vision of a child telling him to 'take up and read', which he took to mean that he must read Scripture.

Personal reflections

There is so much more to Augustine's life than can be written here. Not only was he a teacher of some renown, he was a prolific writer willing to use his experiences as subject matter to explain God's grace. At a time when autobiographical writing was rare, his work is considered one of the first such pieces. Along with sermons, works on doctrine, biblical Scripture and treatises written to challenge the heresies of the time, there is no other Latin author who wrote so profusely. In his *Confessions*, he takes the objective stance of a philosopher considering in detail his motivations for stealing fruit as a boy and why the thrill of doing so was pleasurable. He reasons that the temptation to steal fruit was not because it was likely to taste good; in fact, once he and his friends had stolen the fruit it was thrown at pigs. Stealing was not to satisfy hunger, he concludes, but for the sheer illicit pleasure of doing so and the excitement of being caught. This insight into his own behaviour throughout his life developed into thinking on original sin and the human tendency to gravitate towards wrongdoing. He concludes that all human beings are flawed, and consequently have the desire to dominate. Acceptance of God's unerring love and grace allows true freedom. In his other theological work, *The City of God*, he criticizes the prevalent Roman view that human life can be perfected to enact justice. Augustine denounced this perspective as flawed. In the book, he distinguishes between the City of Men and the City of God, whose founder and ruler is Christ, the personification of true justice.

The search for wisdom still rings true today. It is identifiable in anyone who yearns to know more of the nature of life, love and meaning. Augustine's desire to make sense of his world, despite the chaos around him, is a familiar sentiment. His courage to question, and his persistence, inspire me in my own search for meaning. Unafraid to use the lens of personal experience and to scrutinize his own life for answers, his writing explores fundamental questions about human nature. When reading about his life, the unrelenting quest for God shines through.

His books and other writings express something of the inquisitiveness we have as children but go on to lose once grown. He wrote on everything. We identify with what he himself went through: the desire to find something meaningful and fulfilling, to indulge in pleasure, and the disdain, after a while, for those things that are fleeting and superficial. His many works reflect different facets of his thinking, but for me his sense of purpose and fulfilment through faith can be summed up in this quote:

> Too late I came to love you, beauty so ancient and so new, too late I came to love you. And see! You were within me, and I was outside myself and searching for you there![1]

Stories of conversion to the Christian faith capture our imagination not just because of the dramatic circumstances of those concerned, but because they have something that we identify with. Although each story is unique, they contain elements that resonate with those who read them. The conversion of St Augustine of Hippo was the outcome of a restless heart, a result of a long journey of self-exploration that led him to examine other philosophies, before eventually settling on what gave his life purpose and meaning – the Christian faith. His was not the dramatic revelation of St Paul, but the result of asking questions with breathtaking honesty.

The general assumption is that those who are renowned for their faith come to it easily: that the path to divine revelation is straightforward, navigated with increasing certainty, and that their journey of faith occurs over a short period of time. Nothing could be further from the truth for Augustine. His struggle and extraordinary honesty encourages us all. He was a North African man in a Roman world whose formative experiences of the faith were shaped through his search for understanding, and the patient, persistent prayers of his mother.

Restless hearts

These are the lessons we must learn,
says the sage singing wisdom's song;
that to rise means first to descend, clutching humility.
Listen to her lyrics, he implores,
that walking wide paths are misadventures in missing the point;
that soul hunger does not diminish with sensuality;
instead, gnawing dissatisfaction and insatiable longing result.

Beyond the words, wisdom's melody soars.
A holy mellifluous crescendo
too high-pitched for those who only dwell in the human city.
Her tuneful insights are entwined through transformed lives.
The sage's tune modulated by praise
responds, the humble heart is the foundation for wisdom's
    home.
The peace of God is the lullaby that soothes desire and restless
    activity.

In the last stanza, the wise join
their chorus piercing the clouds,
unlocking glimpses of finger-tip glory.
Frequencies barely perceptible to human ears.
Lyrics weaving hope through despondency
that to be fully alive is to embrace the song of love.

A Prayer of St Augustine

O God, you are the light of the minds that know you,
the life of the souls that love you,
and the strength of the wills that serve you;
help us to know you
that we may truly love you.
And so to love you
that we may truly serve you;
whom to serve is perfect freedom:
through Jesus Christ our Lord.

He, like many before and after him, left his native land to heed the call to somewhere else, to the unknown.

St Hadrian/ Adrian of Canterbury

(c. 630–710)

Sharon Prentis

The influence of North African theologians and Church Fathers such as Augustine, Athanasius, Tertullian, Origen, Clement and Cyril is well known. However, another less well-known scholar who hailed from Africa was Hadrian of Canterbury.

An eighth-century manuscript on church history written by the English St Bede (the Venerable Bede) records Hadrian, also known as Adrian of Canterbury, as being a monk of African origin who was much respected by his peers. Born into a nomadic Berber tribe, he spent his youth in the deserts of North Africa, probably in the region of Libya Cyrenaica. Despite being recognized by the Church with his own feast day, little is known of Hadrian's early life. What is known about him comes from the writings of other early Church leaders and from the personal correspondence between the Anglo-Saxon noblemen and clerics. These paint Hadrian as something of a genius or polymath. Not just a biblical scholar, he was also well acquainted with monastic culture, ecclesiastical rules, Greek philosophy, rhetoric, literature and the sciences of the time. One of his students,

Aldhelm, who later became Bishop of Sherborne, describes him as 'endowed with unutterably pure urbanity'.[1] This image of a nomadic tribesman who embraced the faith, renowned for being erudite and exhibiting a courteous and refined manner, goes against notions of Anglo-Saxon Britain and Africa at the time.

After travelling to Naples from Africa, he devoted himself primarily to biblical studies, then became the head of the monastery on Nisida, a small island in the Bay of Naples, where a strong tradition of biblical scholarship existed. Following a visit to Rome to meet Pope Vitalian, Hadrian was entrusted with several imperial diplomatic missions to France. After the death of the Archbishop-elect of Canterbury in Rome in 667, Pope Vitalian offered him the archbishopric. Hadrian declined, saying he felt unworthy of such an exalted position and was adamant that someone else would be better suited. Pope Vitalian approached Hadrian a second time, ordering him to consider the position. Being mindful of obedience to the papacy, Hadrian provisionally accepted the offer on the condition that he could have some time prior to being enthroned to find someone else more suitable to be consecrated as archbishop. On Hadrian's advice the post was offered to Theodore, a monk from Rome, who accepted the appointment and went on to make a significant impact on the early English Church.

A letter from the Pope stated that the monastery had to be free from secular influence and that the Archbishop should have a special relationship with the abbot, treating him more as a friend than a subject. Bede's history of the early Church indicates that Hadrian wielded a wide influence as a counsellor to both the Pope and the Byzantine Emperor, two of the most powerful people at the time. Though it can be tempting to reinterpret history through a modern lens, turning down the opportunity to become the Archbishop of Canterbury to continue his passion to teach speaks audibly of his modesty.

After the election of Archbishop Theodore to Canterbury, Hadrian was sent to accompany him to England. However, he was detained en route in France on suspicion of being a spy. After a year of captivity, he eventually arrived in Canterbury and was made abbot at the monastery of St Peter and St Paul in Canterbury. Part of his role there was to assist Theodore in his episcopal duties, while also teaching scripture, astronomy, science and maths at the school in Canterbury, which, in Bede's words, 'attracted a crowd of students into whose minds they daily poured the streams of wholesome learning'.[2] The remit of Hadrian's role included not only being the Abbot of Canterbury, papal legate, companion to Archbishop Theodore and teacher, but also counsellor to many of his former students long after they had completed their studies with him. Although none of his writing survives today, he is referred to in early biblical commentaries and other books based upon his teaching at Canterbury and something of his character and his gift as an educator and servant of the Church still resonates. Even down the centuries Hadrian's reputation testifies to commitment, service and the desire to realize the talents of others. He knew what he was created for and had the confidence to pursue it with a single-mindedness born of a dedication to the call placed upon his life. Hadrian was between 75 and 80 years old when he died, being buried in his beloved St Peter and

St Pauls, until his remains were moved to the new buildings in 1091. Hadrian, like many missionary pilgrims before and after him, left his native land to follow the call to another place for a specific purpose: to teach others the Christian faith.

Personal reflections

I first learned of St Hadrian after doing some preliminary research to identify saints from other countries. An internet search revealed thousands of black saints from around the world, most of whom were recognized by the Roman Catholic Church; however, there were a few that were also acknowledged by the Anglican Church, among them being St Hadrian of Canterbury. I was intrigued by why this monk who originated from Africa travelled to England. The journey there from North Africa via Italy must have been arduous, fraught with danger and a step into the unknown.

Hadrian strikes me as a man of integrity with a strong sense of purpose. As an educator, I am intrigued by his insistence on remaining an abbot so that he could teach. Hadrian may not conjure up the same image of holiness as other Church Fathers – little is known of his writing and his influence was confined to teaching others – but those he taught wrote of the impact he had on them. His skills in a variety of subject areas reflect not only versatility but a willingness to engage with knowledge and culture as a follower of faith.

To teach is more than to impart knowledge or skills: it concerns the inspiration of hope and the love of learning. By all accounts, Hadrian was a cultivated man who shared his extraordinary knowledge with others to enable them to understand what was meaningful to their lives. By engaging with the world of his day, Hadrian embodies excellence in teaching as an aspect of being Christ's disciple. He was a man who lived a holy life and who used his great ability to found several schools for the education of young men.

Today, central to the vocation of teaching is still the virtue of inspiring the desire to learn, in the face of challenges, social changes and the increasing recognition that education is not just about maintaining an economic system but helping others realize their potential and become all they are created to be. Schools and universities began as institutions of learning established by the Church, and it is noteworthy that a North African man was instrumental in founding a centre of learning. His task was to place faith alongside reason; to support individuals in developing their potential and in so doing make the kingdom of God real. The significance of St Hadrian's example is in his dedication to his call, which is of great relevance to Christians today. Here was a man who was not a native and who was not defined by who he was or where he came from, but by what he did for others.

Prayer

Heavenly Father,

We give thanks for the example of Adrian who understood what he was made for: to teach, encourage and lead those in the faith.

May his life of dedication and service act as a source to remind us that we are called by you to fulfil our talents for your purposes.

Christ, as God incarnate you made the ultimate sacrifice for humanity; help us not to count the cost but to be aware of the greater gain, that of being with you for eternity. Help us to remember the lives of those who sacrificed everything for righteousness' sake, rather than embrace temporary comforts, because they saw your eternal glory.

May we, like them, come to recognize your sovereignty in every area of our lives. Amen.

Meditation

Called into your extraordinary light, your holy servants were so inspired by your goodness that nothing else mattered. They are caught up in the wonder of you and thereby reflect your glory, so that we in turn are compelled to look in awe at your wonder. As they inspire us by their actions, born out of your inspiring of them, help us to come into the fullness of what you have called us to do.

God raises up saints
from the most unlikely
of places and people.

St Juan Diego Cuauhtlatoatzin

(1474–1548)

Sheila Varghese

Sheila Varghese was born in Bangalore, India and comes from a Kerala Syrian Christian[1] background. After many years in theological and neo-literate education, Sheila worked with the Bible Society translations department and as a columnist and special correspondent for newspapers in India. Her last working years were with social services in the UK.

Sheila strongly believes in inter-confessional cooperation. In a joint project between Protestants and Roman Catholics in the 1990s, she worked together with the late Sr Genevieve de Cordove[2] on a chronologically arranged, condensed version of the Old Testament using the text of the Jerusalem Bible. The publication was for students in Indian schools.[3] Sheila remains keenly interested in bettering the plight of voiceless people.

In 2001, the nearly 10 million indigenous Mexican Indians felt honoured and vindicated when Juan Diego Cuauhtlatoatzin was canonized as the Americas' first indigenous saint. Their fight against centuries of racial discrimination in a land that had been their ancestors' and their home for as far back as they could remember seemed over. However, when the official portrait of the sixteenth-century Chichimeca Indian[4] was unveiled, there was bitter disappointment and a sense of betrayal. For the picture of the saint, reproduced by an artist from hearsay and local legends, showed the saint as a light skinned, full bearded man who looked nothing like an indigenous Mexican, but more like their Spanish conquerors. As Fausto Guadarrama López, a writer in the Mexican Mazajua Indian community who has long spoken on behalf of the indigenous people of Mexico, put it: 'This is disturbing. First we win a moral victory. Then we get this image with Western features. Are they trying to conquer us again through this image?'[5]

Who was the real man behind this misrepresentation? Juan Diego Cuauhtlatoatzin[6] was born in 1474 in Cuauhtitlan. A native of Mexico, he converted to Catholicism together with his wife in 1531 following the arrival of the Franciscan missionaries in Mexico in 1524. He is believed to have had four visions in December 1531. The visions were of Mary, the mother of Jesus, who appeared before him as a dark-skinned Indian at the hill of Tepeyac, which is now within Mexico City. When the local Spanish bishop, Juan de Zumárraga, demanded proof of the apparitions, a miraculous imprint of the image of the Virgin Mary is believed to have been found on Juan Diego's rough cloak. Neither rich nor influential, he is reputed to have been fervent in his religious devotion and respectful and gracious to all.

In the narratives about him only three relatives are mentioned: his wife, María Lucía, a son, and an uncle who was very sick and whom Juan Diego cared for with deep dedication. There have subsequently been those who claim direct descent from him, in particular two eighteenth-century nuns. Following the apparitions, Juan Diego was permitted to live next to the hermitage erected at the foot of the hill of Tepeyac and his life thereafter was spent serving at the shrine there. The Basilica of Guadalupe, one of the world's major centres of pilgrimage for Christians of all traditions, as well as for non-Christians, is said to house Juan Diego's *tilma*[7] (mantle or cloak). Juan Diego died in 1548 at the age of 74.

The life story of Juan Diego is found in an ancient document, the 'Nican Mopohua' (meaning 'Here it is told'). Antonio Valeriano (*c.* 1531–1605) is said to have composed it around

1560, about 30 years after the events themselves. It is generally held that at Valeriano's death the original manuscript was passed to Fernando De Alva Ixtlilxochitl (*c.* 1568–1648) of the royal house of Texcoco, a historian and governor of Texcoco and Tlalmanalco. The manuscript is said to have been held in the library of Real Universidad de Mexico until 1847 when it disappeared. The original text has not been seen since and is commonly believed now to be in some unknown war archive of the US Department of State. However, an informative thesis on an early manuscript dating from 1649 is to be found at the New York Public Library,[8] and of this there are several Nahautl transcriptions and Spanish and English translations.

The Nican Mopohua describes in poetic language the four apparitions Juan Diego experienced. It relates how after each appearance he went to the bishop to relay the message he had received, asking that a place of worship be built at a specified location. The bishop remained aloof and disbelieving, asking for a sign. Finally, during the fourth apparition, which was in winter, Juan Diego was instructed to collect some flowers that were surprisingly growing among rocks. The flowers were placed in his cloak, which, when presented to the bishop, revealed upon it an image of the Virgin Mary. This cloak is said to be the one still preserved today in the chapel at Tepeyac.

Not unlike the lives of other inspired and holy people, including Jesus himself, doubts have been cast by some scholars on whether Juan Diego ever existed, despite the historical evidence and the unwavering faith of the peoples of Guadalupe. Critics have argued that because Catholicism was losing ground in the Americas to other Christian denominations and the violent

Indian rights movement led by Zapatista rebels, the Vatican, in an attempt to reach out to Mexico's Indians, canonized Juan Diego, an indigenous Mexican. At the forefront of critics of the Guadalupe miracle and the historicity of Juan Diego Cuauhtlatoatzin has been the researcher the Revd Stafford Poole. While not doubting the holiness of Juan Diego, Poole questions if he ever existed at all. He calls the tradition 'pious fiction' and prefers to think of it as an outstanding example of the way religious devotion and national identity can be fused together.[9]

The position of the historian David A. Brading, author of a highly sympathetic study of the Guadalupe miracle, is ambivalent. Brading says: 'There is no historical evidence whatsoever that such a person actually existed.'[10] He holds that, the Guadalupe tradition carries a theological truth that cannot be discerned by 'ill-judged questions about historicity, but only by thinking of the image the way Eastern Orthodox Christians think of icons and the way that Catholic theologians now regard many of the miraculous Gospel stories about Jesus' birth'.[11] His indecision is further illustrated in a letter to *The Tablet*, a Catholic weekly, where he calls the story of the visions of Juan Diego 'a sublime parable', and says, 'To canonise Juan Diego makes as much sense, and as little, as to canonise the Good Samaritan.'[12]

Miguel León-Portilla (b. 1926), a Mexican anthropologist and historian, and a prime authority on Nahuatl thought and literature, holds that 'effectively many people were already flocking to the chapel of Tepeyac long before 1556, and the tradition of Juan Diego and the apparitions of Tonantzin (Guadalupe) had already spread'.[13] The chief problem as seen by Poole and

Brading is that, whereas the Guadalupe portrait and devotion surrounding it clearly date back to the mid-1500s, it was not until 1648 that Miguel Sanchez, a Creole priest, published the account. The same account, told more simply and movingly in Nahuatl, appeared a year later in a book produced by a friend of Sanchez. There is also the the Codex Escalada or Codex 1548, a parchment discovered in 1995 by a Jesuit, Xavier Escalada, and published in 1997.

Consequently, the investigations carried out by scholars at the Vatican do not agree with the Poole and Brading theories. That indigenous people have primarily used oral traditions as a way of preserving their history needs to be part of this argument. Documentation of oral traditions is generally a later happening. All of the above leaves us with at least two important questions. First, can what Poole calls 'pious fiction' be changed by centuries of devotion of an indigenous people into what Brading terms 'a sublime parable'? And, second, can the Church insist on historical fact as an absolute? After all, the historicity of the Christ of Christianity has been challenged time and again.

Personal reflections

Mexico is still at the forefront of political debate. Chimamanda Ngozi Adichie, the renowned Nigerian writer, relates how she, on her first visit to Mexico, having bought into the political debate, had taken the default position that all Mexicans were abject immigrants. However, on her first morning there, Adichie explains how she felt ashamed of her own thinking as she saw the Mexicans as a people with their own dreams and ambitions, with their dignity and self-worth intact.[14] As late as 2016, in the US elections, the building of a wall to keep Mexicans out became an election pledge.

In this climate of political and social hopelessness, Juan Diego Cuauhtlatoatzin's importance to the people of Mexico, and all those who feel powerless, cannot be underestimated. He speaks alike in accents that common people going about their business, in the marketplaces and in the tea houses, and those in seats of power in Mexico, can understand. It is the age-old truth: God raises up saints from the most unlikely of places and people.

In February 2016, Pope Francis, on his visit to Mexico, encouraged the people by a moving reflection on the Gospel account of Mary's visit to her cousin Elizabeth.[15] He spoke of Juan Diego, 'a poor indigenous man' who felt worthless, but to whom a sacred mission was entrusted.[16] As Héctor Zagal, the novelist, wrote: 'The great saint of Mexico will be an Indian, who in these times of neoliberal economics would be selling gum on the street and would be written off as an idler by the bourgeoisie.'[17]

Meditation

Some eastern sages follow a star to find a king.
They look for him in the royal palaces and courts
but he is not there!

Some eastern sages follow a star to find a king.
They are led to a manger where beasts of burden
shelter for the night.

Some eastern sages follow a star to find a king.
They find him in a cattle shed,
dank and dark and unpleasantly sultry.
With the rising stench of fermenting hay
and animal dung; a place of mess and filth.
An unlikely abode for a king.

Two brothers, fishermen both of them
going about their daily work,
casting nets into the sea.
Two others, young and fiery, also fishermen,
were doing the same.
They heard an itinerate preacher call to them
(they did not know he was God)
but they left their boats and nets
and still smelling of sweat and fish and salty air
followed him!

Another day, another man.
a tax man this time.
Despised by the masses and hated by all.
Seen as an extortioner, a pariah.
An unlikely candidate for sainthood
is called aside to a special task,
to be a bosom friend of the Messiah.
And on and on throughout the years
from poverty and hunger and hopelessness.
Weighed under serfdom and prejudice;
penury, despair and misery.
The most unlikely people

with the most unlikely backgrounds,
from the most unlikely races,
of the most unlikely faces and colours and creeds,
are called aside to be saints.

And as if to impress on us the benchmark
God descends into an unlikely situation.
Is born into an eastern carpenter's family.
Poor and of a lower caste,
with the seal of illegitimacy stamped heavily upon him.

God of our universe,
throughout the ages
you continue to call ordinary people:
those who are passed by each day;
those who are ignored
and dismissed without a word.
Unlikely people from unlikely places
and races and colours and creeds
God of our universe,
you call them
to be your saints.

He treated all equally, regardless of race or social ranking, always anchored in his deep and strong faith.

St Martin de Porres

(1579–1639)

Joseph Fernandes

Joseph Fernandes was in born in Lisbon, Portugal, to a strict, conservative Roman Catholic family, during the last few years of a dictatorship and the collapse of the Portuguese 'empire'. On his mother's side he is of Jewish and mixed-race ancestry. This has informed his cultural heritage and identity.

Since arriving in the UK over 20 years ago, he has had a varied working life, including several years as an estate agent and butler. Today he is, as he says, 'following my true vocation'.

Joseph started the discernment to ordained ministry when he was 13, and eventually became a Dominican friar at 18. However, he later decided to leave this way and live the life of a lay person. This was not the end of his story. In 2015 he became a curate, and the following year was ordained priest.

Joseph is an active member of the Anglican Minority Ethnic Network (AMEN) and the Churches Network for Gypsies, Travellers and Roma (CNGTR).

St Martin de Porres (Juan Martin de Porres Velázquez) was born on 9 December 1579, in the city of Lima, Peru, during the Spanish occupation. Born illegitimately to Don Juan de Porres, a Spanish nobleman, and Ana Velázquez, a freed black slave, his father abandoned the family after his sister was born. Ana, his mother, tried to overcome poverty by taking in laundry but eventually could no longer support him. He was placed with a barber, who was also a surgeon, in order to learn medical arts.

Martin used to spend many hours praying during the night, and as he got older this practice increased. As an African descendant he was not allowed to join a religious order, and instead at the age of 15 asked the Dominicans of the Convent of the Holy Rosary in Lima to accept him as a *donado*, a lay brother. In return for the privilege of wearing the habit and living with the religious community he had to perform menial tasks in the monastery. However, he did not abandon his old trades of barbering and healing. It is reported that he was harassed both before and after joining the monastery, harassment which may have been racially motivated. It is said that when he was cooking, the monks would hide the kitchen's pot-holders, and one of the early stories surrounding him was that he could pick up the pots with his bare hands without being burned. He also displayed self-denial and a determination to identify himself with the lives of Peru's indigenous people who lived in poverty. A few years later, the Prior of Holy Rosary gave permission for Martin to take vows as a member of the Third Order of St Dominic. This decision was not well received by all the friars, mainly because he was illegitimate and descended from slaves, with some calling him a *mulatto dog*. Soon after, at 24, Juan Martin was allowed to profess religious vows as a lay brother, but never to become a priest. He was placed in charge of the infirmary, a role he held until his death.

Martin's care for the sick was well known, and his superiors saw in him the virtues necessary to carry out the difficult but vital role of looking after the infirmary. In fact, he also provided for the sick outside the convent, and his ministry extended, without distinction, to both Spanish nobles and slaves. It was not long before miracles were attributed to him. Martin's life reflected God's extraordinary gifts: ecstasies that lifted him into the air, light filling the room where he prayed, bilocation, miraculous knowledge, instantaneous cures. He had a remark-able way with animals, from those working in the fields to rats of the kitchen (as illustrated in a Legend of the Rats), keeping several cats and dogs at his sister's house.

When an epidemic struck Lima, Martin transported the sick to the convent until his superior, alarmed by the contagion threatening the friars, forbade him from continuing such dangerous activities. In the end, his sister offered to take in those who were being turned away from the convent, which still incurred the disapproval of his superiors. He argued that the precept of charity took precedence over that of obedience and was eventually allowed to exercise his ministry. Several of his fellow religious brethren took him as their spiritual director, but he continued to call himself a 'poor slave', not allowing his ego to be swayed by a lack of humility. He was a formidable fundraiser, obtaining funds for dowries for poor girls, so that they were able to marry or enter a convent. He also founded a residence for orphans and abandoned children.

After being ill for a year, with agonizing pain, Martin died on 3 November 1639, at the age of 60. He had won the affection and respect of many of his Dominican brethren and people beyond the confines of the convent. He was known for his miracles and people claimed he was a saint. After his death there were many claims of miracles performed and graces received. He was beatified in 1837 and canonized in 1962, and was designated the patron saint of universal brotherhood. His feast day is celebrated on 3 November.

Personal reflections

In terms of a legacy, Martin de Porres is a famous figure within Latin American Catholicism, and began to receive renewed attention in the later years of the twentieth century. This is partly due to his mixed-race background, as he is one of a comparatively small number of Catholic saints who could be classified as black. He treated all equally, regardless of race or social ranking, always anchored in his deep and strong faith. He was clearly a religious leader with a perennial appeal to the popular imagination. His sometimes defiant, but not arrogant, attachment to the ideal of social justice for those of shared heritage has achieved deep resonance with a church, and society at large, attempting to carry forward such an ideal in today's modern world. The values Martin stood for were as relevant in his own time as they are now, and these can be witnessed in some of his concerns relating to black people and people of multiple heritage: for interracial justice, social justice, race relations and racial harmony. In Martin de Porres we find a fitting patron of Christian forgiveness for those who are discriminated against, and Christian justice on the part of reformed racists. One person can indeed make a difference, as witnessed in the life of Martin de Porres.

Martin de Porres has been for me the embodiment of standing alongside the disenfranchised and the marginalized, and of promoting interracial and social harmony. When I first came across his life, I was a young and impressionable Dominican friar, firmly believing I could change the world and make it a better and more equal place. What struck me about Martin was that despite all adversities, and against all odds, he was able to rise above racial hatred, social injustice and inequality and make a significant difference to the lives of those living on the fringes of society. I could not have asked for a better role model. His life has inspired me to trust God implicitly and to exercise a ministry focused on servanthood.

Prayer

Loving God, we thank you for the life of Martin de Porres, and we prayerfully lift up our hearts filled with serene confidence and devotion. Mindful of his unbounded and helpful charity to all levels of society and also of his meekness and humility of heart, we offer our petitions to you. Show to the people of every race the paths of unity and of justice, of love and compassion, that your servant Martin displayed throughout his life and ministry. May we too become beacons of hope to others, in a world that acknowledges personhood and justice. We ask this so that through mutual benevolence in you humankind may increase the fruits of grace and merit the rewards of eternal life. Amen.

In creating the first
religious congregation
for indigenous women
he created a space
in which women's
spirituality, faith
and dignity could be
recognized and flourish.

St Kuriakose Elias Chavara

(1805–71)

Tricia Hillas

Born in Kuala Lumpur, Malaysia, the Revd Canon Tricia Hillas is of
dual heritage – Asian and white British. She finds that this invites
reflection on what it means to live at the confluence of different
cultures. In recent years she has been exploring this reality and has
been delighted to have visited relatives far and near, since her close
family extends across Malaysia, Japan, Australia and Great Britain.
Strikingly, a recent gathering of first cousins included Anglicans,
Roman Catholics, Muslims and Buddhists.

Prior to ordination in 2002, Tricia was a social worker alongside
people living with HIV & AIDS, young adults with disabilities
and people with 'challenging' behaviour. In addition to her present
role as Canon Pastor of St Paul's Cathedral, London, she serves
on the national council of the Committee for Minority Ethnic
Anglican Concerns and is Dean for black, Asian and minority ethnic
communities for the Two Cities Area in the Diocese of London.

Travelling through the Indian state of Kerala you can't help but notice emblazoned on road signs and billboards the slogan adopted by its tourism department back in the 1980s: 'Kerala: God's Own Country'. Here my grandfather, Payadakan Kunjamboo Nambiar, was born.

Decades afterwards, I visited the state that raised him. Taking to the gentle backwaters, in a small craft capable of navigating waterways too narrow for the larger houseboats, we arrived at Chavara Bhavan, in Kainakary. This shrine, set amid lush coconut palms and verdant paddy fields, encompasses the ancestral home and birthplace of St Kuriakose Elias Chavara. We were the latest of the thousands of people each year who come to pray in this sacred place, still accessible only by boat.

Chavara was born in the small village of Kainakary on 10 February 1805. He belonged to the Syro-Malabar Catholic Church, which traces its origins back to the ancient Christians of Kerala, said to have been baptized by St Thomas the Apostle.

He was the youngest of six children, the devout faithfulness of his family profoundly influencing Chavara's own faith and ministry. In adulthood he described how as a child he grew under the care of his mother who first taught him to pray.

> Sitting at her feet I slowly began to know God. Even when she woke up to pray at midnight and prayed on her knees, I too was beside her on my knees and learned from her lips the names of Jesus and prayers to the Mother of God.[1]

Soon he enrolled at the village school, studying languages, arithmetic and elementary sciences under the guidance of his pious Hindu teacher, Asan. If his home life imprinted on him the significance of family, and his years at the village school the significance of education, then his encounter with Fr Thomas Palackal would underscore the impact that a priest can have on someone exploring their own vocation and path in life. A young teenager when he sensed the call of God, Chavara entered seminary in Pallipuram in 1818. There Fr Palackal's life of asceticism, his earnestness in acquiring knowledge and his zeal for the salvation of others profoundly affected Chavara, who resolved to seek to grow into the likeness of Christ.

Chavara almost didn't complete his training. Not long after he entered seminary his parents and only brother died in a smallpox epidemic. Deeply grieving, Chavara returned to his village. Many advised him to abandon his vocation and stay. It was a terrible dilemma. After much prayer, Chavara entrusted all the family property to his elder sister, settled the family's affairs, and returned to continue his studies.

On 29 November 1829, at the age of 24, Chavara was ordained priest. He presided at the Eucharist for the first time at the Chennankary church, dedicated to St Joseph, where he had been baptized. It is said that all of Chennankary village flocked to attend the Mass officiated by their 'little Kuriakose'.

From the beginnings of faith, at his mother's side, Chavara took his own spiritual formation and interior life very seriously. Through prayer, solitude, scriptural reading and study, he sought wisdom and intimacy with God. His work, *Atmanuthapam*, is marked by deep gratitude and a hunger to be ever-refined by Christ. In it he speaks of the tender relationship to which God invites us: 'Meditation is conversation with God. As you would with a friend, you sit close to God, moved by love, intimately communicating with Him.'[2]

Chavara's profound mysticism was expressed outwardly in his writings. He wrote in at least five languages – Sanskrit, Syriac, Tamil, Latin, Italian, and his mother tongue Malayalam. In his poetry he sought through familiar phrasing to draw people deeper into their own spiritual life. His minor epic poem *Anastasyayde*, for example, takes up the rhythm of the songs of the local boatmen.

Chavara was concerned not only for the individual but for the collective life of the Church, her unity, mission, people and priests. A reformer, he founded and ministered at the first seminary for Syrian Christians in Kerala. Crucially this was a house for laity as well as priests, and would combine spirituality with service to the community. After his death on 3 January 1871, Chavara would eventually be laid to rest here. He also co-founded the first congregations for indigenous men and women. Chavara had a strong conviction that men, women, priests and laity alike should be resourced and renewed in their

faith. In a time when sermons were uncommon he emphasized the proclamation of the word, but only after meditation,
reading and study. What was to be preached was to come from
the heart and soul, not merely from the lips. He revised and
renewed the liturgy. He was not afraid to stand against disunity,
or to chastise churches – even with the threat of closure – when
they failed to grasp the vision of serving their communities.

Unsurprisingly, Chavara's whole-life approach to faith provided practical guidance akin to a rule of living.[3] His wisdom
included much on family life: 'Gentle words to children carry
more weight than high-sounding outcries.' '[Parents] develop
[children] in a regard for truth and justice.' And on the manner
in which Christians are to live, he said: 'Don't humiliate a poor
man, nor create difficulties to him, because if God happens to
see their tears, surely he will question you.' 'The day in which
you have done no good to your fellowmen will not be recorded
in your book of life.'

The conviction that inner faith is to be lived out for the bene-
fit of others found expression through Chavara's ministry in a
variety of ways. As Vicar General of the Syrian Catholic Church
he promoted the creation of schools attached to churches. These
contributed to the high literacy rate still enjoyed in Kerala
today. Chavara arranged for the provision of study materials,
clothing and meals for children from the poorest backgrounds.
Most significantly, Chavara decreed that parish schools should
admit children from all religious and caste backgrounds. The
importance of this could be missed, unless it's remembered
that at the time Dalits[4] lived as bonded labourers, forced to
work without wages. Rules restricted their movement in public

spaces, including denying them the right to draw water from the same wells as others. They were, however, welcome at Chavara's schools.

Chavara's reforming inclusion extended to women at a time when the sphere of their influence remained primarily within the home. As a child, Chavara had benefited from the strength of a devout woman; in establishing the first religious congregation for indigenous women he created a space in which women's spirituality, faith and dignity could be recognized and could flourish. He encouraged these women to develop their ministry and to exercise leadership outside the convent too, by offering education and vocational training for other women in the neighbourhood.

Faith also took tangible form through the foundation of a house for the sick, destitute and aged, which opened at Kainakary in 1869. The first of its kind in Kerala, it inspired other similar houses and came about because of Chavara's galvanizing of the parishes under his oversight. This inspiring of a collective response to need is further exemplified by the practice of *Pidiyari*, a distribution system by which Chavara encouraged people to set aside one handful of rice each time they prepared rice for themselves. This set-aside amount was gathered and distributed to those in need. Chavara recognized and taught the value of small consistent life sacrifices and choices woven into everyday life.

A man of steely courage and divine understanding, Chavara's contemplative practice enabled him to envision new possibilities for the common good. A poet of the divine presence, he brings together in our imaginations the Christ of justice and of intimate communion.[5] Towards the end of his life, Chavara, losing his physical sight, retained an intense desire to see God:

> When my eyes are closed upon the whole world,
> Grant, O Lady, I may see the face of God your Son.[6]

Personal reflections

In many ways it has been hard to get to know St Chavara. There are many differences between us: he a nineteenth-century male Syrian Catholic priest; I, a twenty-first-century Anglican woman priest, writing continents apart. Reliant on secondary sources, I am aware that many of these come with the glow of hagiography. My contemporary mind, used to flawed heroes, even heroes of faith, wants of course to know other things, such as what he found difficult, when he despaired, how the parishes reacted when he insisted they 'get with the programme'.

Despite all that is unknown, the waters of Kerala unite us and what draws me most to St Kuriakose Elias Chavara is the profound interplay between his interior and exterior worlds, between contemplation and action. The Eighth President of India, R. Venkataraman, put it this way:

> Few people have been able to combine the contemplation of God with the service of man as naturally and creatively as between the world of faith and the world of action. Father Chavara represented both. A mystic, he could also be an engine of activity. Capable of withdrawing into his innermost being, Father Chavara was at the same time a motive force for the establishment of a social order in which everyone could live in dignity and faith.[7]

I began by referring to the slogan I saw displayed on so many Keralan road signs:

'Kerala: God's Own Country'. Other signs for shops and businesses also caught the attention: 'The Holy Family Travels and Transports', 'Mary and Martha Textiles', and my very favourite, 'The Infant Jesus College of Engineering'. How wonderful to be surrounded by reminders that God is as interested in the everyday aspects of our lives, education and work as in the worship we offer. Chavara urges us towards an integrated faith, modelled on the life of the One born into a human family, who called his followers 'friends', invited them intimately close and sent them out to heal and bless others. I believe that Chavara is a saint for this present age, when increasingly people seek an experience of divine nearness,[8] which, being rooted in honest, vulnerable openness to God, is made real in daily life, giving rise to authentic living, beyond the boundaries of ourselves.

Prayer

Generous God, we give you thanks for the example of Kuriakose Elias Chavara, whose intimacy with you gave rise to compassion for those longing for hope and led to the renewing of your Church. Enable us so to see you, that we too are moved by your compassion and set free to serve you in our neighbour. May the streams of contemplation and action meet in our lives as they did in your servant Chavara. Amen.

In a world that is often suspicious of 'the other' and hostile towards those who are different, Ceferino attempted to alleviate tensions through holiness and servitude.

Blessed Ceferino Giminéz Malla

(1861–1936)

Steven Horne

Raised in a single-parent family in often challenging conditions, Steven was brought up as a Christian by his mother, who taught him how to use Christianity as a means of survival. After a brief stint in the armed forces, Steven married aged 20, and spent the next 11 years working in various positions – from a police officer to a bank clerk – while raising a family of six children.

In 2011, despite having very few qualifications, Steven secured a place at university, studying for a degree in theology and religious studies. With a strong work ethic, he graduated with first-class honours and, thanks in part to original work presented in his undergraduate dissertation on Gypsy beliefs, he was awarded a fully funded PhD scholarship.

Now aged 36, Steven has written a highly original thesis devoted to a new way of understanding Gypsy and Traveller culture – a 'Gypsy theology'.

In May 1997, Spanish Gypsy Ceferino Giminéz Malla – or El Pele, 'The Strong One' – was beatified by Pope John Paul II. Four others were also recognized for their Christian servitude that day, but Ceferino's inclusion was particularly special, for one significant reason: Ceferino was the first (and only) person of Gypsy origin ever to be honoured as a saint.

He had lived a life of devotion to his faith, and paid the ultimate price in 1936, facing a Spanish firing squad for defending priests from attacks and for refusing to cease his habit of prayer. Typically, the history books revere El Pele for the way his life ended. While it was his act of martyrdom that secured him recognition by the Church many years later, it was his life of integrity, honour, loyalty and holiness that secured him recognition among his own people, the Gypsies. In a life spent healing the divisions between Gypsy and gorger (non-Gypsy),[1] Ceferino succinctly combined both the particularism of his Gypsy ethnicity and the universalism of his Christian faith, dedicating himself to healing the hearts and minds of all he encountered; he is indeed a saint among his people as well as his Church.

I first encountered Ceferino during a period of research for my undergraduate degree. His story jumped from the pages as I eagerly sought examples for my final-year dissertation, entitled 'What Gypsies Believe and Why it Matters to the Church'. Ceferino and I shared a common pursuit – to bring understanding and reconciliation between Gypsies and non-Gypsies. In a world that is often suspicious of 'the other' and hostile towards those who are different, Ceferino attempted to alleviate tensions through holiness and servitude. It is for this reason that to an unfamiliar and arguably forgotten and despised people, Ceferino the Gypsy is both important and inspirational.

I had spent a lifetime encountering first-hand the hostilities between the two cultures; however, I experienced the troubles from both 'sides'. My mother is a gorger or non-Gypsy, and my father is a Romany Gypsy. They had met under peculiar circumstances, during my father's period of national service in Cyprus. The two would eventually divorce, resulting in a situation that would include homelessness, social exclusion and poverty. As a result I essentially grew up within two cultures, an amalgamation of Gypsy values and 'settled' practices. I would all but leave school at the age of 15 to work with my brothers in their landscaping business; money at that stage meant food on the table, which carried more value than qualifications. As a response, much like Ceferino, my Christian faith and my character evolved, both in practice and in nature.

There are several accounts that speak of the reputation Ceferino had for being honest, for being a good mediator and for being generous. But one event has proved to be particularly encouraging – for myself, for GRT (Gypsy, Roma and Traveller) individuals and for those seeking to build bridges between communities and peoples. The account I allude to is for all intents and purposes the Gypsy equivalent of the good Samaritan (Luke 10.25–37). The story starts with a local landowner who suffers an attack in the road – not by bandits or thieves, but from tuberculosis. Ceferino encounters the man, and rather than passing by and ignoring him – for fear of contagion – he chooses instead to stop and help him. Ignoring his own safety, comfort and business, Ceferino hoists the suffering landowner on to his shoulders and proceeds to carry him home. After attending to the man's needs, Ceferino is eventually financially rewarded by the man's family, a blessing that would ultimately enable Ceferino to start a business, in what was a period and a place of financial instability and uncertainty.

The selfless actions of Ceferino on that day were entirely countercultural and unexpected, particularly from a 'Roma' or Gypsy. In that one example, faith triumphed over fear, and love conquered hate. Ceferino's submission to his calling to be an example of Christ's love in the world, and his understanding that he and others were children of God, proved in the immediate circumstances to be tangibly rewarding. Many years later, his example would continue to bless and encourage others – including me. Ceferino's beatification at last gave hope to Gypsies, Roma and Travellers, that they had finally been recognized for who they were in the eyes of God, rather than in the imaginations of human beings.

Ceferino had a habit of turning what seemed mundane into the exceptional; he had no children, he mostly worked as a businessman and he was quiet and well dressed. Yet through these 'normal' life choices, he was already shattering the stereotypes that suggest a Gypsy will have many children, will only perform manual work and will be 'dirty'. Through individuals like Ceferino, these hurtful and harmful ideas that have dogged GRT people for centuries were being challenged head-on. Ignorance, however, continued to prevail. Nevertheless, Ceferino's sincere application of faith every day made the difference. The socio-political world of his day stood no chance in resisting a sincere Christ-filled person, determined on showing love to all. Jesus himself had provided the blueprint of selfless love. History would later provide more examples through persons like Martin Luther King Jr, showing how loving and living as Christ had done could force tangible change in social climates and political atmospheres where oppression reigned and inclusion was absent.

Personal reflections

While Ceferino's impact at the time was arguably limited, the potentiality of his example was given new life through the recognition afforded his legacy by Pope John Paul II. The beatification allowed for his story to be remembered and retold by a community whose history, fables and traditions are passed on orally. It seemed as though the trail had gone cold on tales of

Ceferino's doings, but where there is God there is a way. Gypsy culture has survived, evolved and endured for hundreds of years; its stories and its heroes are no exception. Modern communication methods such as the internet have provided platforms upon which Gypsy stories like Ceferino's can be collected and shared; he may not be around to see it, but his descendants are here and are hearing.

Much of Gypsy culture is focused on heritage and family. Whether passing traditions to the next generation or honouring events and people of the past, survival of the collective is paramount, and sharing memories and inspirational accounts is part of that process. Ceferino is inspirational because he demonstrated to his own people that survival and progress do not have to be internalized. Conversely, to thrive physically and spiritually, one must face outwards rather than inwards. Through Christ, he could accomplish this. He never compromised his Gypsy values and traditions, and never hid his ethnic identity. Rather, he used what he had and who he was to show others in his community and beyond what they could be.

It could be argued that the way Ceferino conducted his life was amazing – that it embraced his ethnic identity yet went beyond it. There was nothing that made it exclusively 'Gypsy', other than the fact that Ceferino was a Gypsy. This is true – but it is a wonderful truth. Through Ceferino's 'normality', he broke down further barriers (as he had always intended to do), to show that we are alike; we are all human. He never once denied who he was, yet he was never limited by what others thought he should be; he understood who he was in Christ. And perhaps in his death and through his beatification, Ceferino beautifully demonstrated for us a valuable, timeless and paradoxical message for our very human struggle to find our place on this earth and in this life: we are many tribes, but through Christ we are one voice.

A reflection on Gypsies and Travellers

> And the king will answer them, 'Truly, I tell you, just as you did it to one of the least of these who are members of my family, you did it to me.'
> (Matthew 25.40, NRSV)

During 2015 (and beyond), European television screens and newspapers were filled with images of social devastation, as the displacement of millions of people created a sea of refugees that poured into Greece and up through Hungary and Germany. Tensions grew, as a revival of nationalism – spawned by fear and fuelled by suspicion – clashed with those who sought to give refuge to their fellow human beings. If only those same television crews had been in southern Greece 500 years previously, they would have witnessed a near-identical mass of unfamiliar humanity arriving on those same shores and following those exact same routes, as Romany Gypsies fled from certain death.

Sometimes our fear of what *might* be can hinder our reaction to what *is*. Just as the Syrian refugees received a mixed reaction, so have Europe's Roma, Gypsy and Traveller populations. Jesus recognized this 'selective' favouring when he posited himself as a criminal (Matthew 25.36, 39), providing a stark reminder of the principle that how we treat our fellow humans is how we treat Christ; love, it would seem, is not negotiable (John 13.34). As a Gypsy, it is sometimes culturally and socially challenging to embrace and be embraced by a culture that has historically mistrusted you. And likewise, it is difficult as someone outside of a minority group to love those who are different – especially if you cannot change or direct them. But that is not our concern. Our concern is to love: to love unconditionally, to love indiscriminately, to love as God first loved us.

Effective mission allows for an encounter between the gospel and culture.

Ini Kopuria

(c. 1900–45)

Sharon Prentis

Few twentieth-century Christians have the distinction of being commemorated by the Anglican community around the world for their role in founding a religious order. Ini Kopuria, a native of the Solomon Islands, was one of them. His vision of Christ in 1925 led him to form the Melanesian Brotherhood (also called Retatasiu) to serve the people of the islands, not following the traditional European fashion of religious communities but in ways consistent with the native cultures, traditions and customs.

Born on the island of Guadalcanal, Ini was sent away to be educated on neighbouring Norfolk Island at a young age. Fellow school students remember him as a quiet, contemplative individual who refrained from the usual boisterous playground activities, preferring instead the pursuit of native games. He had a reputation, even as a youngster, for being mindful of others, defending the younger boys from the high-spirited play of the older ones. A competent student, Ini was destined to have a similar life to his peers; however, recognizing his nature and the way he worked with others, he was encouraged by his teachers to become a catechist – a religious teacher to his native people. Ini, though, had other things in mind; because of his great love of adventure and travel, he chose to join the Solomon Islands' police force, which was one of the few career options open to Solomon Islanders at the time. It was a job in which he excelled, rising rapidly through the ranks to the position of Police Sergeant. It was expected that he would have a distinguished career in the police service. However, that dream came to an abrupt end when he was involved in an accident while attempting to make an arrest. As a result of his injuries, Ini was admitted to hospital, remaining there for some time. It was while recuperating that he had a vision of Christ encouraging him to relinquish his career to pursue a more purposeful one. A letter sent to his bishop following the event reflects his change of mind:

> God has called me from following that manner of life, and in my pain and sickness God has shown me that I should see clearly that it is not [my duty to live] as a policeman, but to declare the kingdom of God.[1]

Soon after being released from hospital, the question uppermost in Ini's mind was how he was to fulfil what Christ was calling him to. His first impulse was to go to the Bishop of Melanesia, John Steward, who, after hearing about the vision and Ini's conviction that he was to serve his fellow islanders, sent the young Melanesian away with his blessing to study theology. It was an environment in which Ini thrived. While at college, discussions with one of his tutors further reaffirmed his sense of call. It was there that Ini heard about St Francis of Assisi, the monasteries of Europe and spirituality in religious communities. These accounts of the religious life – the sense of purpose, their contemplative practices, the centrality of prayer and heart for mission – further convinced him that God wanted him to serve others in keeping with those traditions, and, more specifically, to serve the indigenous people of his native island, Guadalcanal, in practical ways that also took account of their culture. Despite decades of white missionaries coming to the islands from overseas, the Melanesian Anglican Church had long recognized that there needed to be a more effective approach to indigenous mission. Geographically, the island archipelago, situated east of Papua New Guinea, was difficult terrain for the white missionaries to navigate. It consisted of six major islands and over 900 smaller islands inhabited by half a million people, and the islanders were not used to travelling out of their compounds on the main islands. The other islands also had their own distinctive identities, languages, traditions and cultures, making them a difficult place to undertake mission.

Most of the overseas missionaries rarely travelled to the other islands, let alone to their interiors, while several islands occupied by the native Melanesians were difficult to reach by boat. In addition, the variety of Melanesian languages and lack of trained indigenous people were also challenges to missionary efforts. What Ini proposed was an eminently practical but simple solution: a band of missionary brothers who would go out into the areas where English missionaries could not travel, offering practical help, spiritual support and encouragement to native islanders. At a formal gathering of the faithful, Ini was admitted as the first Elder Brother. As well as devoting himself to the work, Ini gave the Brotherhood use of his land to provide food.

The Brothers' work was guided by a set of simple principles: first and foremost, to preach Christ to unbelievers while living in small communal 'households' of between four to eight Brothers. Each household would nominate an Elder Brother or Father to oversee the work. Brothers took vows of poverty, obedience and celibacy, which were renewed yearly. There was no requirement to take a life vow, which allowed individuals to serve for a specific period rather than their whole lives. There was no expectation that they would remain there for life. Vocational gifts were stressed rather than the usual education qualifications. Communal life was an important aspect. Brothers worked in pairs and moved every three months to encourage the formation of independent lay communities who became responsible for their own spiritual life, with the clergy acting as advisers and guides when necessary. Ini Kopuria knew the importance of transmitting the gospel in a language and culture familiar to the people. How else would native islanders learn about their faith unless it was relayed in ways that were culturally relevant without compromising belief.

Ini's early death at the age of about 43 was a great loss to the Christian fellowship. Sad as it was, it did not diminish the work of the Brotherhood. The impact of his endeavours still continues today as the Brotherhood carries on its mission work among the islanders. The Melanesian Brotherhood was innovative in that it did not just seek to replicate religious communities, but adopted practical approaches be fitting a multicultural society. The Brotherhood has been described as one of the most outstanding indigenous movements in the Church throughout the Pacific.[2] Such was their unique approach to indigenous mission that it has been adopted by other religious communities. Continuing the legacy of being relevant to the societies in which they serve, the order founded the Sisters of Melanesia in 1979 to work with the women of the islands.

Personal reflections

From all accounts, Ini was a modest man, quiet, reflective and unassuming. Yet he is not only remembered for founding the Melanesian Brotherhood, but for being instrumental in bringing the Christian faith to Melanesia. Like the historical religious orders originating in the Middle Ages, founded by men and women from European culture, the Brotherhood had a visionary from the heart of its community who was prepared to relinquish what was dearest to him for a greater cause. By recognizing that he could do something for his own people he took inspiration from the past and interpreted the principles for his own context.

It is very seldom that we consider the complex process of ensuring cultural relevance and the importance of honouring those things that form an essential part of our identity. Ini understood that, and his life reflected a sincerity to preach the gospel among his own native people in a way that made sense to them. An important lesson for all contexts is that effective mission allows for an encounter between the gospel and culture.

Through his role in the Brotherhood, Ini demonstrated that Christianity can be presented in culturally relevant ways.

The mission of God enfolds culture, picking up on the redemptive analogies[3] that each culture contains and that allow for greater understanding. That is what Christ did; he went where people were and presented the gospel in ways they could understand. I am struck by how simple, practical and yet profound this approach is.

Prayer

Almighty God, you inspired your servant Ini Kopuria to declare the kingdom of God to the indigenous peoples throughout the Solomon Islands.

We give thanks for those called, like the Melanesian Brotherhood, to live in community with an emphasis on fellowship and proclaiming God's love.

Move us by the Holy Spirit to bring your good news in relevant ways to everyone.

Inspire your Church to communicate in ways to reach all people who are created in your image.

Strengthen those who work to preach the gospel of Jesus Christ. May we also feel so inspired to boldly proclaim to those who are unaware of your grace; through Jesus Christ our Lord. Amen.

An entire nation identified itself with this unremarkable Christian nun from a hitherto unknown township in Kerala.

St Alphonsa

(1910–46)

Sheila Varghese

I was just seven years old, but I remember the incident like it was yesterday. My parents returned to our modest home in South Asia having just been to the cinema or 'flicks', as we called it back then in the mid-1950s, and my mother proceeded to relate the plot of the film they had just seen: *The Song of Bernadette*.

My mother was a great storyteller. Her stories were intensely colourful, minutely detailed and in keeping with the culture of the Indian subcontinent, always interlaced with several other narratives. So, my mother, as was her wont, digressed, relating to us the tale of another young woman, much like Bernadette, who lived in a town less than 30 kilometres from our ancestral home in Mallapally, Kerala, India. Her name was Anna; she became a nun and took the name Alphonsa. Sr Alphonsa was later canonized, becoming the first Indian woman to be thus honoured.

St Alphonsa was born on 19 August 1910 in Kudamalur in Travancore district in Kerala state, which lies in the southwest of India. Her parents were Syrian Christians (Nasranis);[1] her father, Cherian Ousep of the Muttathupadathu family, and her mother, Mary Puthukari. St Alphonsa was named Anna at birth, but as is usual in Kerala she was affectionately known by a diminutive of her name, 'Annakutty', meaning 'little Anna'.

Annakutty, the fifth and last child of her parents, was born in the eighth month of her mother's pregnancy. It is believed that Mary Puthukari's premature labour was caused by the fright she received when a snake wrapped itself around her while she was asleep. Her mother died when she was just three months old.

Annakutty's infancy and early childhood was spent in the home of her grandparents in Eluparambil, Kerala. Her grand-mother, a pious and charitable woman, imparted to her the importance of faith, prayer and acts of kindness and charity to the poor and less fortunate. She was baptized and became a communicant according to the Syro-Malabar rite.

Annakutty's earliest education was undertaken by her great-uncle, Fr Joseph Muttathupadathu. Later, she attended the elementary school of Thonnankuzhy, where her particu-lar friends were Hindu children. Two of her classmates, now in their late nineties, speaking after her canonization, recalled walking with her to school. They remembered her as a very kind child, but deeply reflective and serious.

In 1920, on completing junior school, Annakutty moved to live with her aunt, Anna Murickal, who was known as a very strict woman. Being unable to discern that the child Annakutty was drawn to a religious life, she was keen to discharge her duties by having her niece advantageously married. During this period Annakutty, who was just 13, fell into a pit of burning paddy husks and injured her feet, leaving her with a perman-ent disability. It is said that this accident was self-inflicted to avoid the marriage. However, accidents of this kind were not uncommon, as open water wells and deep pits for burning refuse were part of the farming landscape.

In 1927 Annakutty joined the Franciscan Clarist Congregation and began her secondary schooling. A year later, on 2 August 1928, on the feast of Alphonsus Ligouri, she entered a religious order, taking the postulant's veil and the name Alphonsa of the Immaculate Conception. On 19 May 1930 she became a novice of the congregation, taking her first vows as a religious nun on 11 August 1931. Her motto was 'Holiness through lowliness'. At the age of 26, while she was desperately ill, Alphonsa testified to having had two visions of St Kuriakose Elias Chavara,[2] which relieved her distress.

Alphonsa's life was marked by physical sickness; she endured multiple medical conditions, including organ wastage and a malignant tumour. In 1940, she was frightened by a thief and remained in shock for nearly a year, afterwards being unable to read or write. As a result, she could not carry out her duties as a teacher and was assigned to the lesser tasks of an assistant teacher, catechist and letter writer. Realizing very early that her ministry was to be one of her own suffering and intercession for the suffering of others, she wrote in her spiritual diary:

> I do not wish to act or speak according to my inclinations . . . No matter what my sufferings may be, I will never complain and if I have to undergo any humiliation, I will seek refuge in the Sacred Heart of Jesus.[3]

To her spiritual director she wrote: 'I feel now that God has intended my life to be an oblation, a sacrifice of suffering' (20 November 1944).[4] Shortly before her death she wrote: 'I have given myself up completely to Jesus. Let him please himself in his dealings with me. My only desire in this world is to suffer for the love of God and to rejoice in doing it' (February 1946).[5] She died on 28 July 1946 in Bharananganam.

On 2 December 1953, Cardinal Tisserant[6] inaugurated the diocesan process for her beatification, which was declared on 8 February 1986 by Pope John Paul II. Fifty-five years later, on 12 October 2008, Pope Benedict XVI, announcing her canonization at St Peter's Square, Rome said:

> This exceptional woman . . . was convinced that her cross was the very means of reaching the heavenly banquet prepared for her by the Father . . . [Her] heroic virtues of patience, fortitude and perseverance in the midst of deep suffering remind us that God always provides the strength we need to overcome every trial.[7]

In India, a country steeped deep in religious tradition, but where just a little over 2 per cent of the population is Christian, this honouring of one of her daughters was a matter of national pride. The ceremony in Rome was attended by a delegation of senior politicians and church dignitaries.

At Bharananganam, at a special Mass attended by people of all faiths and none, an entire nation identified itself with this unremarkable Christian nun from a hitherto unknown township in Kerala. The late Dr A. P. J. Abdul Kalam, a former President of India, a scientist by profession and a Muslim by faith, speaking at this gathering, delivered a universal and yet theological discourse on the salvific nature of suffering. He said:

> I ask myself what spiritual life inspired Sister Alphonsa? Here I would like to remember a great biblical event, where Jesus Christ was crucified. On the day of resurrection Jesus says, 'Oh humanity, I have glad tidings for you.' This is a great message of forgiveness and love. In Sister Alphonsa we see such a spiritual awakening.[8]

Her grave at St Mary's Forane Church in Bharananganam remains to this day a place of pilgrimage and miracles. Her birth centenary in 2010 was marked with commemorative coins.

Personal reflections

Growing up in a country plagued with poverty and misfortune, but where belief in God was a given, and religion a part of culture, left me convinced that suffering was a sign of God's favour. For is this not exemplified in the life of Christ and in that of holy people?

However, as a young student of theology in the late 1960s there came a radical shift in my thinking. Prosperity theology was catching on in India. Poverty, misfortune and suffering were now equated with God's disfavour.

I have spent a good part of the last 30 years trying to unpick a lot of this thinking. For, neither of these two positions is absolutely true – nor untrue. As Dietrich Bonhoeffer observes, God meets us in our need; but equally, when we meet God we do so when God is in need.[9] Both receiving.

Thoughts on God's endless mercy[10]

Mercifully you shut the pages of tomorrow,
and the day after;
so that we may know it is you who lets
the sun rise on every new dawn.

Mercifully you allow a lion cub
to fall to its death.

Foreseeing that it may be
the cause of death itself.

Mercifully you allow evil men
to remain;
so that good men may become better
and remain humble.

Mercifully you water the
negativisms of yesterday;
to show us our need of you
to make us positive thinkers.

Mercifully you bring those little accidents our way:
a bruise, a tear, or the taps running dry.
To teach us that as ever,
you remain the provider.

Mercifully you send us
a pitch-dark night.
To awaken in our senses
our need of you.

Through all our days,
mercifully you show us one step ahead.
For our human frailty cannot take
the sheer exhilaration of the goodness
you in your mercy store for us.

Pauli Murray lived a faith that was not afraid to challenge the most powerful ideologies of her day.

Pauli Murray

(1910–85)

Rachel Laurence

Rachel Laurence is a poet and teacher based in Huddersfield, West Yorkshire, where she was born in 1965. Rachel is passionate about the potential for the Holy Spirit to transform both people and culture, and works alongside those of all faiths and none to achieve this end. She has a teenage daughter, a cat and a dog, who continue to be her inspiration and an (apparently) willing audience for the fruits of her creativity.

As a child at Sunday school, saints were to me inspiring and unusual people who led unconventional lives. To my five-year-old imagination, martyrdom was a strange concept. The heroic aspect of selfless acts of devotion appealed to me, but I wasn't sure if I would ever have the heart to die for my faith, especially if it would mean never eating ice cream again! 'Will there be ice cream in heaven?' I wondered.

I was brought up in a non-Christian household where my faith ebbed and flowed depending on the ups and downs of daily existence, with scant input from Sunday school and my well-thumbed copy of the Ladybird book, *Jesus the Helper*.

As a Christian I am walking the walk with Jesus. It looks a little different to the floating through life's trials and tribulations that I once expected; one step forward, two steps back, stumbling, bumbling, 'Jesus, where are you? Phew! Please don't leave me to walk on my own again! Well not for too long. Yes, I know you were with me all the time, well, I know it now, but back there . . .?'

I am fascinated by those people, ancient and modern, who lived and worked among the messiness and complexity of the world and who often came from unpromising backgrounds to achieve much through God's infinite grace. One such person is Pauli Murray, an African American priest and Civil Rights activist who was canonized by the Episcopal Church in 2012.

Pauli was brought up by her aunt and grandparents after the early death of her mother at only four years old. Her father also died a tragic and violent death in 1923 when she was just 13.

Not one to recoil from the challenges she faced as a black woman in the early decades of the twentieth century, she came up through college, working to support her studies before, due to the economic depression of the 1930s, abandoning them to go and work as a teacher in a remedial reading project in New York City. At this time, she also had articles and poems published in magazines. Through her work in the Civil Rights Movement she developed a lifelong friendship with Eleanor Roosevelt. Around this time (1938), she campaigned to enter the all-white University of North Carolina, but it wasn't until 1951 that the first black person was accepted.

She studied law at Howard University and at the same time helped to set up the Congress of Racial Equality, a pacifist organization advocating non-violent civil disobedience. After graduating from Howard University and being rejected on grounds of gender from Harvard, she eventually continued her studies at California Boalt School of Law.

An Episcopalian all her life, she contemplated ordination after promptings from various people, until she eventually entered the ordination process and in 1977 was the first black woman to be ordained in the Episcopal Church.

Throughout her life, Pauli Murray lived a faith that was not afraid to challenge the most powerful ideologies of her day. This faith informed the work she did through a deep concern for equality and inclusion. She faced discrimination of all kinds, mainly on grounds of race and gender, and also struggled with her own sexual identity and explored this with honesty, insight and integrity.

Pauli Murray died of cancer in Pittsburgh on 1 July 1985. Sara Azaransky, in her book *The Dream Is Freedom: Pauli Murray and American Democratic Faith*, which looks closely at Murray's writings, states: 'For Murray, salvation entailed the power and possibility of transforming the world and of restoring creation.'[1] Azaransky described Murray as a 'significant twentieth-century African American intellectual who grounded her calls for democratic transformation in Christian concepts of reconciliation and of the coming kingdom'.[2]

Personal reflections

Pauli Murray was unknown to me when I embarked on the search for a saint. I knew I wanted to write about a female saint, preferably one who had been alive and walking on this planet at the same time as me. The more I read about the life and work of Pauli Murray, the more astounded I was at the fact that I had never heard of her before, such was the significance of her involvement in and contribution to the Civil Rights Movement of 1950s and 1960s America.

There are many things to admire about her life: the fact that she came from very humble origins to become a lawyer, priest and poet; the way that her faith was inextricably entwined with social justice; her strong sense of inclusion and equality, inseparable from the biblical Scriptures and revelation of the Holy Spirit, which were undoubtedly the driving force behind her relentless thirst for peace and reconciliation; the way that she carried within the cells of her body the two races she spent her whole life trying to reconcile, being the great-granddaughter of a slave owner and a slave; the fact that she never gave up fighting for what she felt was central to her faith, despite many setbacks and being on the receiving end of race and sex discrimination herself.

On reading her autobiography, the lasting impression is of a life constantly moving on to face the next challenge. The narrative of her life seems not to fade out but to stop abruptly, only to continue, one imagines, in 'the next room', talking and walking with her Father. As a saint's life should, she compels those of us who walk this earth now to take up that narrative and embody its influence in our lives, to continue it on in some way.

Her example inspires me to keep pushing for the things in my life and the lives of those around me that are important – truth, justice, fairness – and not to give up, no matter how hard circumstances become. I wish I had known her earlier in my life, but knowing her now makes me thankful that she lived the life she did in partnership with the Father. For that, I will be for ever inspired.

Prayer

Lord, as we walk along the narrow way with you, help us always to be outward-reaching, forward-thinking, unconditionally loving. Thank you that despite our weaknesses, and often because of them, you can turn our messy, faltering lives into examples of your caring, loving, restorative presence in the world. Amen.

Sr Marie-Clémentine's motto in life was 'to serve and bring joy'.

Blessed Marie-Clémentine Anuarite

(1939–64)

Michelle Bartholomew

Dr Michelle Bartholomew was born in Yorkshire into a devout Roman Catholic, African Caribbean family. After a number of years working for the community in the health sector, Michelle embarked on a teaching profession.

Michelle is a Senior Lecturer within the School of Human and Health Sciences at the University of Huddersfield. Her research interests include religion, ethnic and cultural identities and how these shape and influence individuals' perceptions of health, Western healthcare and medical practices.

As an active member of the Roman Catholic Church, Michelle particularly enjoys her work with a Mothers' Prayer Group. This international group devotes time through prayer, reflection and recital of the Holy Rosary for the needs of children throughout the world.

It was in the year 2016 that I first chanced upon the Blessed Marie-Clémentine Anuarite. I had always known that I shared a birthday with St Thomas Becket, but was completely unaware that I also shared it with another holy person. Discovering that I shared a birthday with Marie-Clémentine compelled me to find out more.

Both St Thomas Becket and Blessed Marie-Clémentine Anuarite died at the hands of soldiers because of their faith. St Thomas Becket was canonized by Pope Alexander in 1173 and is known as 'the protector of secular clergy'. Many pilgrims visit his shrine in Canterbury Cathedral in the UK. Blessed Marie-Clémentine Anuarite was beatified in 1985 by Pope John Paul II, an event witnessed by both her parents. She was canonized in 1999. Her life story, showing her strength of faith and love, has been a deep source of inspiration for me and many individuals, particularly those living in the Congo who are trying to recover from years of suffering and hardship.

Anuarite Nengapeta was born on 29 December 1939 in Wamba in the Belgian Congo. Her father was Amisi Badjulu, her mother Isude Julienne. She was the fourth of six children, all girls, and was given a name rich in meaning that truly resonates with her life and untimely death: 'An', which means one who does not fear, and 'uarite', derived from the French word *lutte* which means to fight.

From the moment she was baptized, Anuarite showed a deep faith in God, a faith that developed and became the driving force of her life. As a young child Anuarite was known for being energetic, strong willed and sensitive. She used to enjoy seeing people and making them smile. Often she would sing and dance to the sounds of cheers and laughter. At the age of 15, Anuarite felt the calling to become a nun, and although this was against her mother's wishes, she ran away to a convent. Initially, her mother tried to get her to return home, but she was determined. Anuarite's mother soon realized that she could not change her daughter's mind and thus reluctantly accepted Anuarite's decision. Anuarite finally took her vows and became Sr Marie-Clémentine in 1959. Despite her daughter's religious calling, Sr Marie-Clémentine's mother tried again to get her daughter to return home and help with the younger siblings. However, Sr Marie-Clémentine refused and, clearly showing her commitment to God, replied, 'Whoever puts his hand to the plough and looks back is unworthy of the kingdom of heaven and sorely offends God.' Sr Marie-Clémentine had such devotion that she intended to follow the Lord unreservedly.

As a nun, she spent much time writing and it is through her notes that we can learn of her innermost thoughts. Sr Marie-Clémentine was devoted to the Blessed Virgin Mary and prayed the rosary every day. At times this was with her fellow sisters or with the children she was looking after. Often she could be seen in deep prayer by a statue of the Mother of Jesus. She knew of the power of prayer, those special times when she had private union with God, and she knew that prayers were a meaningful directive for her daily actions.

Sr Marie-Clémentine enjoyed helping and caring for others and being a role model and mentor to other nuns. She took great pleasure in teaching, looking after young children, being attentive to their needs and making others happy. Indeed, Sr Marie-Clémentine's motto in life was 'to serve and bring joy'.

In 1964, there was a rebellion in the Congo, with many rebels believing that all monks and nuns were allies of the foreigners. One of the rebel leaders named Olombe had seen Sr Marie-Clémentine and he wanted her as his wife. However, as we have seen, Sr Marie-Clémentine was devoted to our Lord Jesus Christ and categorically refused his advances. In order to try and get Sr Marie-Clémentine to change her mind she was isolated from other nuns and threatened with violence, but she remained defiant. At her refusal, the rebels, under the command of Olombe, beat and stabbed her. During this physical abuse, she continued to resist and pray, saying, 'I forgive you for you know not what you are doing.' Sr Marie-Clémentine was then shot by Olombe and died from her injuries on 1 December 1964.

When the civil war was over, Olombe was captured, condemned to death and imprisoned for his atrocities. He spent five years in prison before he was eventually pardoned and released by the new president. Upon his release from prison he returned to his Catholic faith, but was now a beggar. When

Pope John Paul II made his visit to Zaire, a newspaper editor found Olombe, and shared with the Pope Olombe's repentance and desire for forgiveness. Sr Marie-Clémentine's parents had already forgiven Olombe, and during her beatification Mass the Pope also forgave Olombe, saying, 'And I myself, in the name of the whole Church, forgive you with all my heart.'

Personal reflections

Throughout Sr Marie-Clémentine's life, she showed a deep devotion, commitment and love for God. We can see that she had many wonderful traits, and the most poignant one for me was her ability to forgive her attacker.

Forgiveness and kind acts towards others form the basis of many theological teachings. However, forgiveness can be difficult at times. Sr Marie-Clémentine prayed regularly, realizing that it is through prayer that we can overcome negative emotions. Sr Marie-Clémentine further showed us that granting forgiveness does not in any way condone the actions of the perpetrators or relieve the hurt and pain; rather, it can instil in one a sense of inner, moral peace, while positively maintaining spiritual health and well-being. Following Sr Marie-Clémentine has heightened my propensity to forgive, however elusive forgiveness may appear in instances of great challenge.

In today's society where there are many injustices, it can be difficult to consider forgiveness. The story of Sr Marie-Clémentine is important because it shows how she epitomizes to the extreme this core Christian principle. We can admire Sr Marie-Clémentine and take her as a role model, as she clearly represents the Christian community by her words, actions and holy fidelity to the Lord. She was a remarkable individual, a martyr who gave up her life for God. However, we must not forget those other holy individuals who are not known to the masses, those known only to the people whose lives they have touched and have had an impact on in some way.

Prayer

We thank you, Lord God, for the life and witness of Sr Marie-Clémentine. Instil in us, as you did in her, your spirit of forgiveness.

Righteous Lord, may we always call to mind that when you were reviled, you did not retort, but committed to the Father those who persecuted you. Open our hearts and minds freely to forgive those who sin against us, remembering always that you have forgiven us.

Give us your grace to stand firm in our faith even in the face of injustice and when we are sorely misunderstood. May our lives continuously influence others for good. Amen.

Holiness is not dependent on status, ethnicity, culture, gender, ability or age, but God's grace.

Conclusion

Sharon Prentis

Called to be saints

From the stories told in the previous chapters the individuals mentioned wholeheartedly embraced the call to holiness. In living with divine purpose, their stories show that holiness is not dependent on status, ethnicity, culture, gender, ability or age, but on God's grace. In essence, it is God's gift of sanctification to us. So, why is it important that we need a diverse range of people in the grand narrative of the Christian faith?

As an awkward teenager, I was not particularly interested in holiness nor had I any desire to explore faith, but the story of Joan of Arc captured my imagination. During the Hundred Years War, at a time of great oppression, the young Joan was an inspiration of hope to the beleaguered people of France, and to me. What impressed me about her story was that she was of a similar age to me when she began her crusade. Joan, guided by divine visions and despite fierce opposition, counselled the heir to the French throne in battle. She was eventually burnt at the stake for heresy, and was only exonerated and made a saint after her death.

In those crucial teenage years, when my sense of identity and purpose was beginning to emerge, Joan's story of courage and conviction spoke to the angst I felt about being young and not heard, and her bravery impressed me deeply. The fact that Joan had a cause to fight for resonated strongly with my teenage self. Would I have the courage of my convictions before those who were more powerful and influential? Was there something that I was uniquely tasked to carry out? Could I stand my ground in the face of opposition? In her story I found something of my own. Although her youth resonated with me, I wondered if there were others from a similar cultural background to myself whom I could identify with. It seemed to my naive mind that because there were no immediately identifiable heroes of the faith, perhaps people like me did not figure greatly in the narrative of faith.

These are typical of two problems when it comes to reflecting on what it means to be holy and on representations of holiness.

First, holiness is confused with human virtue; being godly is based on standards from the prevailing culture rather than seen as being in Christ and a gift from God. Many of us know of someone who communicates something of grace, whose presence exudes a distinctive inspiring quality. It is all too easy to idolize those who appear to have an extraordinary ability and to be specially 'chosen' by God. We can be guilty of reading their stories as heroic tales, superhuman efforts that are out of the reach of ordinary Christians. However, what we find in the written accounts of their lives is that they were interwoven with disappointment, tragedy, suffering, being misunderstood, failure, and tirelessly working without realizing any sense of satisfaction. The stories here are not universally known, with the details forgotten at best or intentionally changed at worst; even so, the grace of God is evident. Here are people of different ethnicities, cultures, backgrounds and eras, whose journeys of faith encompass the experiences of our humanity. Primarily, they are people of God with a peculiar dedication to love him and to love others.

Second, when the lives of holy people are considered, we often fall into thinking that we are so far removed from them in terms of the potential to be used by God. How can we ever be like them? We fail to see that they fully embraced their humanity and surrendered to the love of God. Yet, this way of thinking was not always the case.

In the early years of its existence the Church referred to those who belonged to it as saints. Those first disciples from different nationalities, social classes, ethnic groups and cultures lived in a radical new way that transcended their distinctions. In his letters to the churches in Asia Minor, the apostle Paul addresses those who are sanctified (made holy) in Christ Jesus, called to be saints,[1] as the source of all hope. Persecution of Christians by the Roman Empire followed, and the term became synonymous with those who were martyred or endured harsh treatment for what they believed. Over time, the term was applied less to the majority of believers and increasingly to a select few, in recognition of their martyrdom, special acts of piety, humility, selfless service, exceptional wisdom and miracles. Martyrs of the faith were especially esteemed, their tombs venerated and relics highly sought after as they were seen to be endowed with miraculous qualities. Holiness and other associated virtues became the preserve of the few rather than something that all could attain. The saintly life was held up as an example of grace, purity and sanctification. Holy people became figures to emulate and their representations, pictures and wisdom writings highly treasured as a spiritual resource by the faithful. Stories and images of the pious were drawn from a limited range of cultures. Most were male and hailed from Europe. A few originated elsewhere. Christian tradition made the briefest acknowledgement of the ethnicity, culture and origins of those early Church Fathers such as Augustine and Tertullian, who originated in North Africa but whose pictures took on distinctly European features.

Despite recent attempts to retell history from the perspective of those not traditionally included, the lives of black saints and holy people largely remained unknown outside their cultures and countries of origin. Nevertheless, those efforts to include a range of stories, wisdom writings and images from diverse Christian traditions have led to a renewed interest in their lives, which have much to teach us about what it means as a diverse people to be committed to God.

Learning from the saints

From our modern perspective, holy people can seem quaint or of little relevance. For example, to be modest or display a reluctance to attract social attention has become unfashionable.

Modernity's current obsession with celebrity and fame is a symptom of a human need for validation. In a culture that endorses self-promotion, film stars, pop idols and cultural icons act as a focus for unfulfilled hopes and dreams and fuel a deep desire to be of worth. In stark contrast, the Church has saints and holy people who teach us that fulfilment comes from realizing our God-given purpose; that the life of faith is ultimately defined by and expressed in love; that personal holiness is a journey we are given the grace to make. Saints direct our gaze away from themselves: they are called to be those in whom others see God. Holy people encourage and motivate us to become part of the divine dance with God, the Father, Son and Holy Spirit, which requires only a willingness to learn the steps in order to join in. Looking at their lives we learn a number of things.

First and foremost they were conduits of God's love for others, often in ways that were countercultural. Ceferino Malla was moved to protect those who were threatened and persecuted because of their faith, even at the cost of his own life. Just as Christ came to serve and not to be served, to give up his life in service for others, so too did Ceferino. A significant aspect of his faith was his willingness to pay the ultimate price.

We do not have immunity from the challenges to our faith. A recurrent theme throughout the life stories of these saints is suffering. St Alphonsa demonstrated what it is to be long-suffering by placing her trust in God. She showed great patience and tolerance in spite of long years of pain and illness. Her life is an example of an alternative view, one of the hope that puts eternity in the picture. Alphonsa regarded her troubles as a means to identify with the suffering of Christ and an incentive to pray for others.

Learning to see God in the midst of troubles is difficult, particularly when what is being experienced is the result of the actions of others. The natural human tendency is to complain, retaliate, hold on to grudges or even seek revenge. To love your enemies and forgive those who do wrong takes immeasurable faith. Marie-Clémentine Anuarite's example of forgiveness speaks powerfully to her trust in God. Her story is a strong reminder of the redemptive power of forgiveness and that ultimately we must trust God, especially in times when we are not able to see the bigger picture of God's divine plan.

The pious life is characterized by selfless service and unconditional love. Humility, deference and obedience are the outer adornments they wear. Eschewing promotion and prestige for the satisfaction gained from doing God's work, both St Hadrian and Ini Kopuria gave themselves to their respective communities, expecting nothing in return except the knowledge that they were doing God's will. Their work and reaffirmation of God's ideals for humanity help us recognize that God values every person irrespective of background.

There is a certain poignancy in their actions on behalf of others in times when society encouraged bigotry and social divisions. Recent times have been marked by a discernible rise in hostility towards others based on racial, religious, cultural and lifestyle grounds. The example of Martin Porres is even more exceptional in his time when prejudice towards those who were different was socially acceptable and even encouraged.

Humility comes from appreciating that they could do nothing of themselves. Those like Chavara and Juan Diego remind us that God values the marginalized, the poor and the forgotten.

This reversal of the world's values is at the very heart of the gospel where, in the kingdom of God, real value is placed on those who would normally be viewed as insignificant.

These witnesses to the faith were not impervious to the challenges of their social circumstances, nor were they afraid to go against the expectations and norms of society. It is only through the lens of history that we see just how radical these individuals were. They were people of their time, and yet they often went against the expected ways of behaviour, because their primary inspiration was God. For Pauli Murray, striving for equality was a natural expression of her work as a lawyer, priest and poet. Despite the many setbacks, she continued her work, motivated by a profound sense of justice and righteousness.

In essence, those featured in this book were individuals who knew their purpose, who believed that spiritual transformation began with them, and who when things looked impossible believed in the possibility of spiritual transformation for others. Chavara was moved to embrace those from all walks of life, but particularly the poor. Chavara and Ini Kopuria utilized 'familiar' indigenous or native understanding to present the gospel in a relevant way.

Saints today

The call to holiness is just as important in our time. The all-pervasive presence of social media means that we have instant access to communication from around the world. At the same time, we are presented with images designed to appeal and gratify, that suggest the need for acquisition and constant entertainment. Advertising explicitly focuses on consumerism, where the individual is of primary importance, rather than expressing a widespread concern for others.

Holy people draw our eyes back to the purposes of God: to make disciples, love, inspire and encourage each other in the body of Christ by mutually affirming one another. Their wisdom has its foundation in the dynamic life of the Trinity – the community we are invited to join and to be in fellowship with. Being saintly is a result of a shared recognition of holiness. Belonging to a diverse array of witnesses challenges our tendency towards self-defined piety; it shows us what holiness should look like and, more importantly, that it is based on dependence on God and interdependence on one another. Community is communion with one another, and ultimately with God.

As knowledge has increased so has the desire to search for wisdom and a more meaningful spiritual engagement. People look back to more ancient ways of understanding the world because they recognize the deeper wisdom of God who acted through ordinary human beings in extraordinary ways.

Although the saints in this book were very much of their time, their examples are still relevant today. The landscape of social relationships is continuing to shift. The resurgence of old divisions along socio-economic/religious/cultural and ethnic lines continues to mar our relationships. The proliferation of views based on fear, and the need to protect resources for the global minority rather than ensuring an equitable distribution for all, mean that we have become much more individualistic and insular. According to the writer Alice Walker, 'Anybody can observe the Sabbath, but making it holy surely takes the rest of the week.'[2] Holiness means daring to touch upon the profound mystery of faith that arises from experience, contemplation, reflection and peace, the intuitive reasoning that is founded on the premise that all will be well in Christ.

Those like St Alphonsa, St George and Ini Kopuria were witnesses to the accompanying doubts, uncertainty and difficulties of their times. Their faith in God took precedence over the expectation of others and their testimonies, borne out through the stories of their lives, are still relevant to our modern age when setting time aside to consider what it might mean to receive the gift of holiness.

Primarily, they are people of God with a peculiar dedication to him and to others. There is encouragement in learning about their lives – not a distant otherworldliness but a deep reassurance that God will be with us too, and a realization that he is still in the business of enabling those in his family to do great things. It is by listening to a variety of voices that we hear something of the divine. Holy lives are laid bare as a witness to help us reflect on our own lives and ponder life's deeper question about the inner world we inhabit with God and that causes us to reach out to others. By viewing these diverse icons of virtue through the lens of faith, culture and experience, our aim is to inspire by telling the unfamiliar stories of people who are not unlike us, yet who sought to be fully aware of God in their time, place and culture.

Lawrence Cunningham suggests that saints make the gospel real in ways that are relevant to the culture in which they live.[3] In that sense, the lives of the saints reveal not only insights but an appreciation of what it means to 'imitate' Christ and participate in the eternal reality of his kingdom. Writing about Thomas Aquinas, G. K. Chesterton observes:

> A saint may be any kind of man, with an additional quality that is at once unique and universal. We might even say that the one thing which separates a saint from ordinary men is his readiness to be one with ordinary men.[4]

The men and women identified in this book are not just models of grace and virtue, but even in their diversity were ordinary folk, like you and me, who had a profound belief in Christ and his kingdom. More importantly, they reflect what it is to be human, to suffer and to overcome severe challenges. Their stories are different, but the one thing they have in common is that their lives were transformed by the Spirit of God. In reading about them we join in this universal fellowship that transcends time and space, the community of the faithful as radical witnesses. A diverse array of saints says much about who we are, and more importantly that God's Church is made up of people who journey together, extolling kingdom values and looking to the complete restoration of humanity. Like the early Church, the impact of such intentionality will not be lost on those around us. It is only by working together, allowing for those heart-to-heart encounters on the basis of mutual love and respect, that we can truly acknowledge that we are all made in the image of God.

It is fitting to conclude with St Paul's opening greeting in his letter to the church at Corinth:

> To you who have been called by God to be his own holy people. He made you holy by means of Christ Jesus, just as he did for all people everywhere who call on the name of our Lord Jesus Christ, their Lord and ours.

> (1 Corinthians 1.2, NLT)

Reflections

St George

S t George came from a multicultural background. If he was living in our day, he would be classed as belonging to a minority ethnic community. However, his courage in standing up for his beliefs and being counted is what set him apart.

- What lessons can we adopt from the life of St George, the patron saint not only of England but of several countries around the world, that may help us bring healing to our fractured communities today?

- Throughout history we see that during times of political uncertainty people often turn to narrow nationalistic thinking. Hospitality and tolerance towards those who are strangers in our midst are forgotten, or these strangers are seen as a burden or the cause of our own dilemmas. Is there anything, however small and insignificant, you can do to show people that there is another way, the Christian way?

Abba Moses

To all intents and purposes, Abba Moses came from the 'wrong side of the tracks', living a life of brutality and violence before coming to faith. As a result, it took some time before others were convinced that he had changed his old ways.

- What qualities did Abba Moses show that gave evidence of Christ's transformation of his life?
- Have you experienced a time when you felt that God was leading you in a new direction? How did this feel? What were the things that helped or hindered your willingness to follow?

St Augustine of Hippo

Despite his notoriety as a key figure of the Christian faith, St Augustine's conversion and faith tells of honest struggle, a search for meaning and the persistent prayers of his mother.

- How can we better recognize this struggle in our own lives? Can we in the depths of our honesty come to know better the depths of God's grace?
- For many, the search for meaning to this life continues. How can we draw upon St Augustine's journey for faith to better understand and encourage those around us in their

searching? How can we share our own stories in order to connect with others on a personal level and aid those with a similarly 'restless heart'?

St Hadrian/Adrian of Canterbury

Hadrian declined the prestigious post of Archbishop of Canterbury, one of the most powerful and influential roles at the time, in order to teach and mentor others in the faith.

- What contemporary lessons can we learn from this?
- Take some time to reflect on the dreams and passions that motivate you, or issues that move you. How might these be used in service of the kingdom and to help others know Christ's love?

St Juan Diego Cuauhtlatoatzin

Juan Diego came from a poor and underprivileged background. He found it difficult to find acceptance even with the leaders of the Church. Despite this, he continued to believe in, and try to fulfil, the mission to which he knew God had called him.

- Can you think of any incidents in the Bible where people were mistreated because of their background or the family they came from?
- Think about a time or circumstance in your life when you may have felt that you were not being heard, or you felt you were discriminated against or marginalized. Spend

some time committing this situation, even if it is something that happened a long time ago, to God's keeping.

- Look at the community around you and see if there is even one thing you can do to give a voice to someone who is fearful in the face of poverty, hardship or discrimination.

St Martin de Porres

Martin endured abuse and was victimized for being illegitimate, a descendant of slaves and having a mixed-race heritage. In response to this treatment, he went against the cultural norms by using his skills to help people irrespective of race, status or wealth. By going out of his way to welcome those on the margins of society he changed attitudes.

- What Bible passages come to mind when reflecting on Martin's story? As Christ's disciples, how might we purposely seek to be of service to those who are marginalized or stigmatized?

St Kuriakose Elias Chavara

Chavara sought to meet and to serve God in the individual, family, church and societal spheres of life.

- How balanced does your own encounter with God in these different spheres seem?
- Which of the two streams of mystical, intimate encounter with God and practical service of others for God seems the stronger in your life at the moment? To which might God be directing your attention right now?

- The Letter of James states that 'faith without deeds is dead'. Why might contemplation (faith) need to be married with action (deeds)?
- Chavara spent much time imaginatively reflecting on biblical passages and characters, seeking to identify himself with them and their situations. Examples would include the prodigal son of Jesus' parable, Mary Magdalene at the foot of the cross, the man to whom Jesus entrusted Mary his mother. What place might such imaginative reading have in your own practice? Is there a biblical character with whom you might presently identify?

Blessed Ceferino Giminéz Malla

Ceferino lived a life of devotion to his faith and paid the ultimate price by being martyred. He was recognized by his own people, the Gypsies, because of his life of integrity, honour, loyalty and holiness, and because his life was spent healing the divisions between Gypsy and gorger (non-Gypsy).

- In our society today there are divisions among people and communities along lines of race, religion, politics and social standing. Reflect on your own beliefs and views, and see if these fit in with the Christ way.
- Ceferino understood who he was in Christ. He demonstrated that although we are many tribes, through Christ we are one voice. Compare this thought with the encounter of St Peter with Cornelius in Acts 10 and consider the lessons it holds for us today.

Ini Kopuria

Ini Kopuria's desire was to make the gospel known to the people of the Solomon Islands. His vision was for all the indigenous people of the islands to understand the gospel in ways that were culturally relevant to them.

- In what ways are Christians called to 'translate' the gospel in our communities, schools, workplaces and among family, friends and acquaintances?

St Alphonsa

Alphonsa's life was marked by physical sickness and suffering. She is said to have suffered with multiple medical conditions, including organ wastage and a malignant tumour. Later in life she lost some of her cognitive skills as a result of being terribly frightened. Alphonsa realized very early in life that, while she was limited because of her poor health, she could nevertheless do much through a life of intercessory prayer.

- Try to find examples of intercessory prayer in the Bible. Study in particular the prayer of Jesus in the Gospel of John, chapter 17.
- Consider whether God is calling you to a life of intercessory prayer.

Pauli Murray

Pauli Murray lived a faith that was not afraid to challenge the most powerful ideologies of her day. This faith informed the work she did through a deep concern for equality and inclusion. Pauli Murray faced discrimination of all kinds, but she never gave up fighting for what she felt was central to her faith.

- What has been your experience of any kind of discrimination, and how have you reacted to being treated unjustly? Have you ever tried to stand up for someone who was being discriminated against? Think about how your faith in Christ has helped you in facing such challenges.

Blessed Marie-Clémentine Anuarite

Marie-Clémentine Anuarite's motto in life was 'to serve and bring joy'. Marie-Clémentine suffered greatly for her faith, but she recognized the need for forgiveness, even of those who were violent to her.

- Forgiveness is an important theme that runs through the New Testament. Jesus taught us to pray, 'Forgive our sins as we forgive those who sin against us.' This is a very difficult command to follow. Think of a few instances in your life when you had to struggle with the idea of forgiveness.
- Forgiveness is required in bringing communities together. Is there something in particular that your community is struggling with? Is there scope for changing things by forgiveness, as Christ commanded us to practise?
- In your meditations, consider that forgiveness as illustrated in the life of Marie-Clémentine does not in any way condone the actions of the perpetrators or relieve the hurt and pain. But it can instil a sense of inner peace and help in maintaining spiritual health and well-being.

Notes

Preface

1 Dietrich Bonhoeffer, *Life Together: The Classic Exploration of Christian Community* (New York: HarperOne, 1978), p. 30.

Introduction

1 W. H. Auden, 'In Praise of Limestone' in *Collected Shorter Poems 1927–1957* (London: Faber and Faber, 1966), p. 241.

Abba Moses (330–405)

1 *The Philokalia: The Complete Text, Volume 1*, trans. and ed. G. E. H. Palmer, Philip Sherrard and Kallistos Ware (London: Faber and Faber, 1995), pp. 95–6.

St Augustine of Hippo (354–430)

1 Augustine, *Confessions*, Book 10.XXVII.

St Hadrian/Adrian of Canterbury (*c.* 630–710)

1 Michael Lapidge and Michael Herren, *Aldhelm: The Prose Works* (Cambridge: D. S. Brewer, 1979), p. 493.
2 A. M. Sellar (trans.), *Bede's Ecclesiastical History of England*, The Christian Classics Ethereal Library (London: George Bell and Sons, 1907).

St Juan Diego Cuauhtlatoatzin (1474–1548)

1 See note 36 of 'St Alphonsa (1910–46)' below.
2 Sister Genevieve de Cordove (1919–95) was an artist, a nun of the Salesian Missionaries of Mary Immaculate (SMMI). She was a pioneer in the use of Indian symbols in Christian art.
3 Genevieve SMMI and Varghese Ramasamy (eds), *The Mini Bible: Old Testament* (Indore: Satprakashan Sanchar Kendra, 1991).
4 Charlotte M. Gradie, 'Discovering the Chichimecas', *Academy of American Franciscan History* 51.1 (July 1994), p. 68.
5 Richard Boudreaux, 'Latin America's Indigenous Saint Stirs Anger, Pride', *Los Angeles Times*, July 2002.
6 Cuauahtlatoatzin means 'the Eagle that talks'.
7 A *tilmàtli* (or *tilma*) was a type of outer garment worn by men. It has been documented from the late post-classic and early colonial eras among the Aztec and other peoples of central Mexico.
8 See <www.nypl.org/blog/2014/04/17/nican-mopohua>.
9 Stafford Poole, *Our Lady of Guadalupe: The Origins and Sources of a Mexican National Symbol* (Tucson: University of Arizona Press, 1995).
10 David Brading, *Mexican Phoenix: Our Lady of Guadalupe: Image and Tradition across Five Centuries* (Cambridge: Cambridge University Press, 2001).
11 Brading, *Mexican Phoenix*.
12 *The Tablet*, 20 February 2016, p. 10.
13 Miguel León-Portilla, article in *L'Osservatore Romano:* Weekly Edition in English, (23 January 2002), p. 8.
14 Chimamanda Ngozi Adichie, 'The Danger of a Single Story', TED talk, July 2009.
15 Luke 1.39–45.
16 *L'Osservatore Romano*, Weekly Edition in English, 12–17 February 2016.
17 Héctor Zagal, in *Reforma*, a Mexican newspaper.

St Kuriakose Elias Chavara (1805–71)

1 J. K. Kanjiramattam CMI, *The Pastoral Vision of Saint Kuriakose Elias Chavara*, 2nd edn (Kottayam: Deepika Book House, 2015), p. 21.
2 M. M. Shibu, 'Chavara: The Mystical Flower of Mannanam' in J. Mannarathara (ed.), *The Life and Legacy of Saint Kuriakose Elias Chavara* (Delhi: Viba Books Private Limited, 2015).
3 Gathered in *Sayings of Blessed Kuriakose Elias Chavara*, ed. Fr Vice Postulator, St Joseph's Monastery, Mannanam.
4 Dalit is a term for the members of lower castes in India. It means 'oppressed' in Sanskrit.
5 Paul Thelakkat, 'Spirituality and Poetic Harmony' in Mannarathara (ed.), *The Life and Legacy of Saint Kuriakose Elias Chavara*.
6 Chavara, Concluding Prayer, quoted in Shibu, 'Chavara'.
7 R. Venkataraman, quoted in Fr Z. M. Moozhoor, *Blessed Chavara: The Star of the East* (Kottayam: Deepika Book House, 1993), p. 128.
8 Diana Butler Bass, *Grounded: Finding God in the World – A Spiritual Revolution* (San Francisco, CA: HarperOne, 2015).

Blessed Ceferino Giminéz Malla (1861–1936)

1 The word 'gorger', meaning a non-Gypsy, is a colloquial term. The Gypsies would ordinarily refer to non-Gypsies as being gadjo (feminine = gadji).

Ini Kopuria (c. 1900–45)

1 Margaret Lycett, *The Brothers: The Story of the Native Brotherhood of Melanesia* (London: SPCK, 1935), p. 15.
2 Charles Fox, 'Brothers in the New Hebrides', *Southern Cross Log*, English edn (January 1939), pp. 15–16.
3 Don Richardson, 'Redemptive Analogy' in Ralph D. Winter and Steven C. Hawthorne (eds), *Perspectives on the World Christian Movement: The Notebook* (Pasadena, CA: William Carey Library, 1999), pp. 285–9.

St Alphonsa (1910–46)

1 Syrian Christians (St Thomas Christians) are an ethnic group in Kerala, India. Their origin is traced to the evangelization of St Thomas Didymus, the apostle of Christ, who is said to have come to India in the first century. Their culture has been influenced by the practices of

the Eastern Syrians and Kerala Hindus. They speak Malayalam, the common language of Kerala, with Syriac for liturgical purposes.

2 Kuriakose Elias Chavara was a Syrian Catholic saint and social reformer in India who founded the first religious congregations for men and women, 'The Carmelites of Mary Immaculate' and 'The Congregation of the Mother of Carmel'. There were reports of miraculous favours received as a result of his intercession. See the chapter about him in this book.

3 Vatican News Service, 'Alphonsa of the Immaculate Conception (1910–1946)', *Daily Bulletin of the Holy See Press Office*, 2008 (retrieved 1 December 2016).

4 Beatification speech of Pope John Paul II, <https://web.archive. org/web/20131112121424/http:/www.alphonsa.com/Content-13/ BEATIFICATION.html> (accessed 1 December 2016).

5 See <https://web.archive.org/web/20131112121424/http:/www.alph onsa.com>.

6 Eugène-Gabriel-Gervais-Laurent Tisserant (1884–1972) was a French prelate and cardinal of the Roman Catholic Church.

7 Vatican News Service, 'Alphonsa of the Immaculate Conception (1910–1946)'.

8 Thomas Kuzhinapurath, *Dr A. P. J. Abdul Kalam's Monograph on Salvific Meaning of Sacrifice* (October 2008).

9 See Dietrich Bonhoeffer, *Letters and Papers from Prison* (London: SCM Press, 1953), p. 174.

10 Adapted from Sheila Varghese, 'Inside the Arena: A Psalm of Life', *The New Leader* (Bangalore), 9 March 1986.

Pauli Murray (1910–85)

1 Sara Azaransky, *The Dream Is Freedom: Pauli Murray and American Democratic Faith* (New York: Oxford University Press, 2011), p. 114.

2 Azaransky, *The Dream Is Freedom*, p. 3.

Conclusion

1 1 Corinthians 1.2.

2 Alice Walker, *In Search of Our Mothers' Gardens: Womanist Prose* (New York: Harvest Books, 1983), p. 351.

3 Lawrence S. Cunningham, 'Saints and Martyrs: Some Contemporary Considerations', *Theological Studies* 60 (1999), p. 331. Available online

at: <http://cdn.theologicalstudies.net/60/60.3/60.3.7.pdf> (accessed 10 November 2018).

4 G. K. Chesterton, *St Thomas Aquinas* (San Rafael, CA: Angelico, 2011; originally published 1933), p. 77.

Bibliography

Books and journal articles

Ambec, J. and Christian, G. G. *St. Martin de Porres: In the Service of Compassion*. Chicago, IL: New Priory Press, 2015.

Anon. *Blessed Marie-Clémentine Anuarite Nengapeta: Daily Gospel Reflection*. Notre Dame, IN: University of Notre Dame, 2015.

Azaransky, S. *The Dream Is Freedom: Pauli Murray and American Democratic Faith*. New York: Oxford University Press, 2011.

Batson, M. and Shwalb, D. 'Forgiveness and Religious Faith in Roman Catholic Married Couples', *Pastoral Psychology* 55.2, 2006.

Bhopal, K. and Myers, M. *Insiders, Outsiders and Others: Gypsies and Identity*. Hatfield: University of Hertfordshire, 2008.

Bischoff, B. and Lapidge, M. *Biblical Commentaries from the Canterbury School of Theodore and Hadrian*. Cambridge: Cambridge University Press, 1994.

Bonhoeffer, D. *Letters and Papers from Prison*. London: SCM Press, 1953.

Bonhoeffer, D. *Life Together: The Classic Exploration of Christian Community*. New York: HarperOne, [1939] 1978.

Brading, D. *Mexican Phoenix: Our Lady of Guadalupe: Image and Tradition across Five Centuries.* Cambridge: Cambridge University Press, 2001.

Burnaby, J. *Amor Dei: A Study of St Augustine's Teaching on the Love of God as the Motive of Christian Life,* London: Hodder and Stoughton, 1960.

Butler Bass, D. *Grounded: Finding God in the World – A Spiritual Revolution.* New York: HarperOne, 2015.

Cascales, J. *El Pelé: All the Gypsies.* Klagenfurt: Hermagoras Society, 1997.

Cavalini, G. *St. Martin de Porres: Apostle of Charity.* Charlotte, NC: Tan Books, 1979.

Chadwick, H. *Augustine: A Very Short Introduction,* Oxford: Oxford University Press, 2001.

Chavara, Kuriakose Elias. *Sayings of Blessed Kuriakose Elias Chavara,* ed. Fr Vice Postulator. Kottayam, Kerala: St Joseph's Monastery, Chavara Office.

Chevalier Chacko, K. C. *St. Alphonsa.* 8th edn, Bharananganam, Kerala: Seraphic Press, 2010.

Chesterton, G. K. *St Thomas Aquinas.* San Rafael, CA: Angelico, 2011; originally published 1933.

Christie, D. E. 'The Call of the Desert: Purity of Heart and Power in Early Christian Monasticism', *Pro Ecclesia* 7.2, Spring 1998.

Clark, C. and Greenfields, M. *Here to Stay: The Gypsies and Travellers of Britain.* Hatfield: University of Hertfordshire Press, 2006.

Collins, M. *St George and the Dragons: The Making of English Identity.* CreateSpace, 2012.

Cooney, A. *Saint George: Knight of Lydda.* Saint Marys, KS: Angelus Press, 2004.

Cunningham. L. S. 'Saints and Martyrs: Some Contemporary Considerations', *Theological Studies* 60, 1999, available at <http://cdn.theologicalstudies.net/60/60.3/60.3.7.pdf> (accessed 10 November 2018).

Dempsey, C. G. *Kerala Christian Sainthood.* Oxford: Oxford University Press, 2001.

Dempsey, C. G. 'Lessons in Miracles from Kerala, South India: Stories of Three "Christian" Saints', *History of Religions* 39.2, 1999.

Drews, A. *The Christ Myth*, trans. C. D. Burns. London: T. F. Unwin, 1910.

Fahlbusch, E. *The Encyclopaedia of Christianity, Volume 5.* Grand Rapids, MI: Eerdmans, 2008.

Fitzgerald osa, A. D. (gen. ed.). *Augustine through the Ages: An Encyclopedia.* Grand Rapids, MI and Cambridge: Eerdmans, 1999.

Garcia-Rivera, A. *St. Martín de Porres: The 'Little Stories' and the Semiotics of Culture.* Maryknoll, NY: Orbis Books, 1995.

Bibliography

Genevieve SMMI and Varghese Ramasamy, S. *The Mini Bible: Old Testament*. Indore: Satprakashan Sanchar Kendra, 1991.

Good, J. *The Cult of St George in Medieval England*. Woodbridge: Boydell Press, 2009.

Gradie, C. M. 'Discovering the Chichimecas', *Academy of American Franciscan History* 51.1, July 1994.

Gretsch, M. *The Intellectual Foundations of the English Benedictine Reform*. Cambridge: Cambridge University Press, 1999.

Hadrian 2 at Prosopography of Anglo-Saxon England. <www.pase. ac.uk/>.

Hancock, I. *We Are the Romani People*. Hatfield: University of Hertfordshire Press, 2013.

Holbock, F. *New Saints and Blesseds of the Catholic Church, Volume 2: 1984–1987*. San Francisco, CA: Ignatius Press, 2003.

Inina. *Ira Retatasiu*. British Solomon Islands: Melanesian Mission Press, 1939.

Kanjiramattam, J. K. *The Pastoral Vision of Saint Kuriakose Elias Chavara*. 2nd edn, Kottayam: Deepika Book House, 2015.

Kearns OP, J. C. *The Life of Blessed Martín de Porres: Saintly American Negro and Patron of Social Justice*. New York: P. J. Kennedy and Sons, 1937.

Kenrick, D. *The A to Z of the Gypsies (Romanies)*. Plymouth: Scarecrow Press, 2007.

Kirwan, C. *Augustine* London: Routledge, 1989.

Knowles, A. and Penkett, P. *Augustine and His World*. Oxford: Lion Publishing, 2004.

Kochumuttom, T. *Blessed Kuriakose Elias Chavara*. Mumbai: St Paul Press, 2014.

Lapidge, M. *The Anglo-Saxon Library*. Oxford: Oxford University Press, 2006.

Lapidge, M. and Herren, M. *Aldhelm: The Prose Works*. Cambridge: D. S. Brewer, 1979.

Lawless, G. *Augustine of Hippo and His Monastic Rule*. Oxford: Clarendon Press, 1987.

Lycett, M. *The Brothers: The Story of the Native Brotherhood of Melanesia*. London: SPCK, 1935.

Macdonald-Milne, B. *The True Way of Service: The Pacific Story of the Melanesian Brotherhood 1925–2000*. Leicester: Christians Aware, 2003.

Mannarathara, J. (ed.). *The Life and Legacy of Saint Kuriakose Elias Chavara*. Delhi: Viva Books Private Limited, 2015.

Bibliography

Markus, R. A. (ed.). *Augustine: A Collection of Critical Essays*, Modern Studies in Philosophy. Garden City, NY: Anchor Books, 1972.

Mendelson, M. 'St Augustine', *The Stanford Encyclopedia of Philosophy*, 2000, available at <https://plato.stanford.edu/entries/augustine/> (accessed 21 December 2018).

Mosconi, G. *Blessed Marie-Clémentine Anuarite: Jesus Alone*. New Bedford, MA: Academy of the Immaculate, 2009.

Palmer, G. E. H., Sherrard, P., Ware, K. (trans. and ed.). *The Philokalia: The Complete Text, Volume 1*. London: Faber and Faber, 1995.

Panthaplackal, T. *Chavara, the Patron of Families*. Kottayam, Kerala: St Joseph's Monastery, Chavara Office.

Poole, S. *Our Lady of Guadalupe: The Origins and Sources of a Mexican National Symbol*. Tucson: University of Arizona Press, 1995.

Raj, V. R. *Stars on the Indian Horizon*. Jaipur: Vivek Prakashan, 2014.

Riches, S. *St George: Hero, Martyr and Myth*. Stroud: History Press, 2005.

Rohr, R. *Simplicity: The Freedom of Letting Go*. Rev. edn, New York: Crossroad Publishing Co., 2003.

Ruggles, R. *Apparition Shrines. Places of Pilgrimage and Prayer*. Boston, MA: Pauline Books and Media, 1999.

Scaria, M. and Joseph, B. 'The Legacy of Kuriakose Elias Chavara as a Social Reformer', *International Journal of Scientific and Research Publications* 5.7, July 2015.

Schweitzer, A. *The Quest of the Historical Jesus*, trans. W. Montgomery. London: A & C Black, 1910.

Sellar, A. M. (trans.). *Bede's Ecclesiastical History of England*, 4.1–2; 5.20. The Christian Classics Ethereal Library. London: George Bell and Sons, 1907.

Slapak, O. *The Jews in India: A Story of Three Communities*. Jerusalem: The Israel Museum, 2003.

Stace, C. *Our Darkest Knight: St George Patron Saint of England*. London: SPCK Triangle, 2003.

Taylor, B. *Another Darkness, Another Dawn: A History of Gypsies, Roma and Travellers*. London: Reaktion Books Ltd, 2014.

Walker, A. *In Search of Our Mothers' Gardens: Womanist Prose*. New York: Harvest Books, 1983.

Way, Y. *Anuarite Nengapeta Marie-Clémentine 1939 to 1964*. Bunia, Democratic Republic of Congo: Institut Supérieur Théologique Anglican, 2001.

Williams, R. 'Christ-Centred Concreteness: The Christian Activism of Dietrich Bonhoeffer and Martin Luther King Jr.', *Dialogue: A Journal of Theology* 53.3, September 2014, available at <http://onlinelibrary.wiley.com/doi/10.1111/dial.12115/pdf> (accessed 30 May 2016).

Wortley, J. 'Discretion: Greater Than All the Virtues', *Greek, Roman, and Byzantine Studies* 51.4, 2011.

Newspaper articles

Boudreaux, R. 'Latin America's Indigenous Saint Stirs Anger, Pride', *Los Angeles Times*, July 2002.

'The Brotherhood', *Southern Cross Log* 32.11, November 1926.

Fox, C. 'Brothers in the New Hebrides', *Southern Cross Log* (English edn), January 1939.

Fox, C. E. 'Ini Kopuria', *Southern Cross Log* (New Zealand edn), 1 June 1946.

León-Portilla, M. Article in *L'Osservatore Romano*, Weekly Edition in English, 23 January 2002.

Staff reporter. 'Catholic Church Celebrates Alphonsa's Canonisation', *The Hindu Newspaper*, 13 October 2008.

Staff reporter. 'City Youth Learn Dying Language, Preserve It', *The New Indian Express Newspaper*, 9 May 2016.

Staff reporter. 'A Place for Those Who Do Not "Count"', *L'Osservatore Romano*, Weekly Edition in English, 15 February 2016.

Steward, J. M. 'The Brothers', *Southern Cross Log* (English edn), 1 October 1926.

Stone, Jon. 'Six Reasons Why St George Is the Perfect Symbol of Multiculturalism', *The Independent*, 23 April 2015. Available at <www.independent.co.uk/news/uk/home-news/st-georges-day-6-reasons-why-st-george-is-the-perfect-symbol-of-multiculturalism-10197345.html>.

Varghese, S. 'Inside the Arena: A Psalm of Life', *The New Leader* (Bangalore), 9 March 1986.

Vatican News Service. 'Alphonsa of the Immaculate Conception (1910–1946)', *Daily Bulletin of the Holy See Press Office*, 2008 (retrieved 1 December 2016).

Vatican News Service. 'Beatification of Father Kuriakose Elias Chavara and Sister Alphonsa Muttathupadathu', *Daily Bulletin of the Holy See Press Office*, 2008 (retrieved 1 December 2016).

Theses

Elizabeth Molly, K. P. 'Religious Philosophy of Blessed Kuriakose Elias Chavara – A Study Thesis', Department of Philosophy, University of Calicut, 2004.

Horne, S. 'What Travellers Believe and Why It Matters to the Church and Educational Providers', BA (Hons) thesis, Canterbury Christ Church University, 2014.

Sermons, addresses and talks

Adichie, C. N. 'The Danger of a Single Story', TED talk, July 2009.

Bar-asher Siegal, M. 'Ethics and Identity Formation: Resh Lakish and the Monastic Repentant Robber', proceedings of a conference in Aix-en-Provence, France, June 2011.

Samasumo, P. 'Blessed Anuarite: Congo DR Prepares the Close of Jubilee Year', Vatican Radio, 2014.

Websites

Benedict XVI. 'Address of His Holiness Benedict XVI: Audience for the Representatives of Different Sinti and Roma Groups', 2011, <http://w2.vatican.va/content/benedict-xvi/de/speeches/2011/june/documents/hf_ben-xvi_spe_20110611_rom.html> (accessed 2 May 2016).

Kuzhinapurath, T. 'Dr A. P. J. Abdul Kalam's Monograph on Salvific Meaning of Sacrifice', uploaded 2008, <www.scribd.com/document/7839320/Dr-APJ-Abdul-Kalam-s-Speech-on-Salvific-Meaning-of-Suffering-St-Alphonsa-Muttathupadath>.

Pontifical Council (PCMIP). 'Nomads: Sinti, Roma – Zefferino Giménez Malla', 2011,

The Tablet, The International Catholic News Weekly, <www.thetablet.co.uk> (accessed 20 February 2016).

<www.vatican.va/roman_curia/pontifical_councils/migrants/documents/rc_pc_migrants_doc_20000601_noma_santi_en.html> (accessed 5 May 2016).

Notes